Bad News

Overwhelming grief swept over me and a tidal wave of emotion poured from my body. I wept uncontrollably before the Lord, facedown on the motel carpet. All I could think about was the time, effort, and sacrifice that had gone into the erection of that building. Literally thousands of people had unselfishly contributed their prayers, financial resources, and physical labor, so Christians in Afghanistan's capital city could have a place to worship the Lord together. Now, three short years after its dedication, the building was being destroyed.

It just didn't make sense.

Afghanistan

The Forbidden Harvest

The challenging
story of
God's work
in a resistant
land.

J. Christy Wilson, Jr.

David C. Cook Publishing Co.
ELGIN, ILLINOIS—WESTON, ONTARIO

Acknowledgments

I would like to express deep gratitude to the following people who have played a role in the publication of this book: my wife Betty who has been an ever-loving partner; our parents and family who have been so supportive; Enid Bate of New Zealand who has given invaluable assistance during research; Holly Greening who has faithfully helped stenographically; Randy Nulton who has edited and rewritten the manuscript; Joe Bayly and Janet Thoma who have also assisted greatly with the editorial process; all in the David C. Cook Foundation and Publishing Company who have made this book possible; Jim Cudney for his photographic ability; the many others who have served in Afghanistan whose names and ministries could not be included in these pages because of space limitations; the trustees of the Kabul Community Christian Church for their faithful support over the years; the trustees of Gordon Conwell Theological Seminary for granting a six-month teaching sabbatical which helped make publication possible.

"For God is not unjust so as to forget your work and the love which you have shown toward His name." (Hebrews 6:10)

First Printing, June 1981.

© 1981 David C. Cook Publishing Company

Published by David C. Cook Publishing Co.
850 N. Grove Ave., Elgin, IL 60120
Edited by Randall Nulton
Cover photo by James Cudney
Cover design by Graphic Communications, Inc.
Printed in the United States of America

ISBN: 0-89191-476-5
LC: 81-67065

Dedicated to the glory of God and to all Christians who have faithfully prayed for or served in Afghanistan; especially those who, like their Master, have sealed their testimony with their blood. These special people include Erik Barendsen from Holland, Eeva Barendsen from Finland, Caesar Mileton from the Philippines, Hans Werner from Germany, Josephine White and Dwight Ritchie from the United States, as well as the Afghan believers who have given their lives for their faith in Jesus Christ.

"Unless a grain of wheat falls into the earth and dies; it remains by itself alone; but if it dies, it bears much fruit." (John 12:24)

Contents

Foreword

When I first went to Afghanistan in 1968, I stopped in India to acquire a visa at the Afghan embassy in New Delhi. It had only been a few years since the Muslim country had changed its policy of geographical and political isolation. Consequently, there was considerable suspicion when foreigners sought visitor's visas. I had to complete a long and detailed application, which called for an almost complete family history and included the name of my employer.

At the time, I was a vice-president of the Billy Graham Evangelistic Association, living in Singapore and directing preparations for the Asia/South Pacific Congress on Evangelism. Even though I knew this information would jeopardize my chances for a visa, I truthfully put it all down.

The young man responsible for granting entry visas scanned my application and then asked me, "Are you going to see Dr. Christy Wilson?"

Surprised, I replied affirmatively.

He handed me a blank form with the suggestion, "I think it would be better if you perhaps used only the initials of your organization, rather than the full name of your employer."

I knew I had found a friend.

When I took the newly completed form back to his desk, I asked, "Do you know Dr. Wilson?"

He smiled as he stamped the visa in my passport, saying, "He was my teacher."

Not this side of eternity will we know the full impact made on Afghanistan by those first "tentmaking" Christian witnesses who went there in the 1950s. Christy and Betty Wilson were the vanguard of a committed company of Christ's ambassadors who volunteered to go and serve both the people and their Lord in Afghanistan.

Until now, this story could not be told because of the extreme sensitivity of the situation. Indeed, telling it would have endangered the lives of those involved. So the workings of God in Afghanistan have been whispered among believers and shared in private prayer letters. Recent events in the country, however, have made it possible for this missionary adventure to be chronicled. Having lived and worked in Afghanistan for over two decades, Christy Wilson is singularly qualified to tell the story.

For anyone who believes in the sovereignty of God, Dr. Wilson's involvement with the landlocked Muslim nation could never be considered accidental. Born of missionary parents in the neighboring country of Iran, the month of his birth was marked by a single missionary event.

Just recounting the story causes me to tingle.

Dr. William Miller, a Presbyterian missionary who was to serve Christ in Iran for forty-three years, had recruited Christy's parents, Dr. and Mrs. Christy Wilson, Sr., to go with him to Iran in 1919. Just a couple of years later, Dr. Miller and some of his missionary colleagues were forced to flee their post at Mashad, Iran, in the face of a threatened Russian invasion. (At this moment in history, we may all be pardoned for a sense of deja vu.)

Because of his burden for Afghanistan, Dr. Miller left the other missionaries for a two-day side trip on foot to a desert area where the Helmand River separates Iran from Afghanistan. He lowered himself into the swirling water and swam to the restricted land on the other side. In recorded history, there had never been a Christian missionary resident in Afghanistan nor were there any known Afghan Christians. Before swimming back to Iran, Dr. Miller plucked blades of grass from the "forbidden" soil and sent them out in prayer letters. Some went to the missionary statesman Dr. Robert Speer with a note: "Here are some of the firstfruits of Afghanistan."

The time was November, 1921—the same month and year when J. Christy Wilson, Jr., made his entrance into the world! Later, Dr. Miller sent one of those blades of grass to the young man so prophetically born.

The story of the penetration of Afghanistan by Christians in the biblical form of "tentmakers" is a missionary saga, made no less so by the fact that it happened in this century instead of some previous one. For one, I am glad it can now be told because today's Christian young people have too few contemporary heroes. As a young person, I used to read missionary books about the exploits of Adoniram Judson, William Carey, John G. Paton, Mary Slessor, and David Livingstone and wonder if the Holy Spirit was doing nothing in my time which was exciting enough to write about.

He was and is, thank God! The stories in this book are a thrilling part of the acts of the Holy Spirit in our time.

W. Stanley Mooneyham
President–World Vision International

1
Miracle over Central Asia

"If you don't know God, come to know him by his power." [*khudawra aga (r) namishnawsee ba qudrateeawish bishnaws.*]

Afghan proverb

6:05 P.M., August 31, 1955. The face on my watch told me something wasn't right. I peered out of the Iran Air DC-3 window expecting to see the familiar barren mountains surrounding Afghanistan's capital and largest city—Kabul. But below stretched pine forest valleys and rugged mountains as far as the eye could see. Suddenly, I realized we were lost! Kabul was at least one hundred miles from the nearest woodlands.

Sitting at the controls of the plane were two Americans. The pilot had never been in Afghanistan, and the copilot was serving as guide without the aid of today's sophisticated navigational equipment. This was his second flight through the Afghan skies.

Somewhere during the course of the scheduled one-hour and forty-five minute flight, our pilot had made a wrong turn. I guessed from the topography of the terrain below that we were probably over the Afghan province of Khost, headed toward Nuristan and the Russian and Chinese border.

I swallowed hard. We were wandering over the jagged central Asian wilderness.

Towering mountains soon dwarfed our unpressurized plane. Banks of pink, billowy clouds loomed thousands of feet above us on the distant horizon. Then the twilight completely disappeared over the edge of the earth behind us. It seemed like we were flying into an endless sea of blackness.

I was airborne because I had accompanied a group of Afghan students to Tehran, Iran. They had boarded a westbound plane to continue their long journey to universities in the United States. Now, I was returning to Kabul to continue my teaching and administrative duties at Habibia College, one of Afghanistan's oldest and most respected schools for high school age boys.

My mind began to stray, remembering a day that had gone from bad to worse. "Mechanical difficulties" had meant leaving Tehran's Mehrabad Airport two hours behind schedule that morning. Scrupulous Iranian customs officials at Zahidan, near the southwestern tip of Afghanistan, had put us further behind schedule. They had insisted that all baggage be taken off the plane and inspected.

The sun was already hanging low in the sky when we had reached our next stop—Kandahar, Afghanistan's second largest city. We had dropped off about a half-dozen passengers, and it hadn't been long before we had been speeding down the Kandahar runway for the final three hundred mile hop of our flight. My watch had registered 4:20 P.M. The pilots had been confident our plane would land and be taxiing toward the small Kabul terminal at dusk. But over Ghanzi they had followed a road heading northeast, paralleling the Pakistan border, instead of taking the northerly jog to Kabul.

The more I thought, the more I realized the next few hours could very well be my last on earth. I knew there were no night landing facilities in Afghanistan, or anywhere else within range of our prop plane. I also knew that the front baggage compartments were stashed with four-gallon gasoline cans. Aviation fuel was not available in Afghanistan at that time, so the plane had to bring in its own supply for the return journey. A crash would mean certain death in a blazing inferno.

I sensed a deep spiritual responsibility to speak with individuals on the plane about their relationship to God. Most passengers I talked to were very receptive. One American, however, cut me short saying, "Don't talk to me about that. When my time comes, it comes; and that's all there is to it!" He turned away and gazed out the window into the night.

I then started a conversation with the Iranian steward. He responded: "I've been to Mecca. Doesn't that make me all right?"

I told him that the important issue now was not where he had been, but where he was in his relationship with God. If he repented of his sins and believed that Jesus had died on the cross in his place, he would receive God's forgiveness. The steward seemed very receptive to what I was saying because he, like the others on the plane, was scared. He knew that the odds of coming out alive were against us.

A little later the steward gave me permission to go into the cockpit. I learned that the only radio contact the pilots had was with Tehran about thirteen hundred miles to the west, and Karachi, Pakistan, an equal distance to the south (Afghanistan airports were not yet radio equipped). The pilots banked sharply to the left, completed a 180-degree turn, and started to follow their flight log in reverse.

It was the only thing they knew to do.

When I mentioned I was a Christian minister, one of the two copilots glanced over his shoulder and said, "Use all the influence you've got!"

"I'm praying," I answered as I turned to leave. "And I know that God is in charge."

I returned to my vacant seat and began to pray. I placed the fifteen lives still on the plane into God's hands. Then I pulled my Bible from my briefcase and wrote this note on the inside front cover:

Dearest Betty, Nancy, Christy, and Martin:

Our pilots have lost their way and it appears that we will crash. I am writing this farewell message in case my Bible is found in the wreckage. I love you more than words can tell.

Put Jesus first throughout your life and serve him faithfully in every way you can. I look forward to seeing you again soon in Heaven. Your loving husband and dad, Christy.

I had just finished signing the note when the corner of my eye caught a reflection off the left wing. We had finally come out of the ominous clouds into clearer weather. A beautiful full moon had risen over the eastern horizon, illuminating the mountains and valleys.

I went back to the cockpit and scouted the silver landscape below. The terrain looked vaguely familiar. I soon recognized a village I had driven through only ten days earlier as I had traveled the bumpy road from Kabul to Kandahar for the funeral of an American engineer. He had drowned in the Helmand River where he was helping to build a dam.

"That town down there is Qalat!" I said to the pilots. I had remembered that Qalat had a spring of water which stands on a hill like an aeropolis. They checked their air map and found our location. From there they headed for Kandahar.

My prayers had been answered. At 8:30 that night we could see the glow of Kandahar's lights in the distance. But the joy I felt was short-lived. Some quick arithmetic told me we had been airborne for more than four hours. We would soon be out of gas.

No sooner had this thought rushed through my mind than the copilot in the jump seat spoke, "We've got to get the airport lit up before we can land!"

"I don't think there is so much as one light bulb at the airfield," I replied softly, hating to reveal the gravity of the situation.

The pilot turned to look at me. "If we can't get it lit up, we'll have to continue flying for Iran!" Then he added solemnly, "But we don't have enough fuel to make it."

How ironic! Even though we had extra aviation gasoline on board, there was no way to get it into the fuel tanks while we were in flight.

Soon we reached the outskirts of Kandahar, and I sighted the Morrison-Knutsen Construction camp. Morrison-Knutsen had been contracted by the Afghanistan and United States governments to engineer an irrigation system in Afghanistan's Helmand Valley. During the 1950s and 1960s, several dams were erected and hundreds of miles of irrigation ditches were dredged in an effort to help the Afghans produce more food in their arid climate. Patterned after the Tennessee Valley Authority, hundreds of Americans were involved in the project at one time or another.

"Why don't we fly low over the camp?" I suggested. "Planes don't fly into Kandahar at night so the noise of the engines will attract attention. The company workers may realize we're in trouble and figure out a way to help."

The pilots made three passes as low as they dared. Within minutes, every jeep, car, and truck on the site was racing to the airfield. Light flooded the runway as the vehicles lined up on each side of the gravel strip. The landing was perfect.

By the time the steward could turn the latch and open the cabin door, our "welcoming committee" had gathered to greet us on the pavement below. Rather than wait for someone to roll up the portable stairs, several of us jumped from the doorway in our haste to thank the group of rugged-looking construction workers who had saved our lives.

One husky American engineer recognized me immediately. "Christy, you mean to say you were on that plane!" he said in disbelief. He engulfed me in a bear hug I shall never forget. We had become acquainted on my recent Kandahar visit. Not only had I conducted funeral services for his friend, but I had baptized his daughter as well.

Morrison-Knutsen's director, T.Y. Johnson, invited every passenger and crewman to a steak dinner at the construction camp. To top it off, they served strawberry shortcake for dessert. Our unexpected hosts also rolled out every spare cot and bed on the grounds as they did their best to convert their simple accommodations into a first-class hotel. The Waldorf Astoria it was not. But no one cared. We were all happy to be alive.

The next day, September 1, 1955, dawned bright and clear. After a hearty breakfast, the construction crew chauffeured us all back to the airport.

My mind again began to wander as we gained altitude and the DC-3 propellers spun us toward Kabul for the second time. Never had I been more grateful for answered prayer. Time and time again, God had reaffirmed my decision to bring my wife Betty to this mountainous, out-of-the-way country in the heart of central Asia where our three children had been born and raised. The miracle of the previous evening had confirmed that God indeed wanted me working and living among these freedom-loving people in "the country of the Afghan."

Little did I realize that a quarter of a century later, this unusual country I had begun to call home, was to become the focal point of world attention. Afghanistan would be locked in a bitter struggle for its freedom.

2
The Iron Claw of the Soviet Machine

"Fear the one who does not fear God." [*az ou kas bitars tki as xuda nanetarsa.*]

Afghan proverb

April 20, 1979 dawned just like any other day in the peaceful village of Kerala, Afghanistan, high in the Nuristan mountains. Women baked bread in brick ovens on the floor of their homes. Children played games in the dust-covered streets. Men caught up on the latest gossip and traded in the marketplace.

The only thing out of the ordinary in this mountain community two hundred miles northeast of Kabul, was the presence of a small Afghanistan army battalion. Led by several "Russian advisors," the gun-carrying troops had entered the village a few days earlier and were patrolling the streets for "security reasons." Inwardly, the independent-spirited citizens of Kerala disdained the Communist-controlled militia. However, people had been able to supress any visible signs of their animosity and were even beginning to get used to the men in uniform.

Then, late in the morning an announcement echoed through the streets from the loudspeaker perched on the minaret of the town mosque.

"Attention. . . . Attention! All men and boys over the age of twelve are to report immediately to the village square."

Seventeen hundred men and boys quickly made their way to

the town center fully expecting to receive *bakshish,* monetary gifts promised by the Afghan government. President Taraki had been using government aid as a public relations ploy to try and quell some of the dissatisfaction with his Communist-controlled regime, especially in the outlying Afghan provinces. The men and boys were aware of this and eagerly awaited their gifts. But what actually happened during those next few minutes is almost beyond description.

The troop commander barked a loud command, and before anyone could react, a barrage of bullets showered the confused mob. The roar of machine guns drowned the screams of agony and terror. Minutes later, when the smoke cleared, all seventeen hundred lay dead or wounded in the town center, victims of one of the world's most ruthless, cold-blooded massacres.

Like clockwork, bulldozers and dump trucks immediately went to work transporting the bodies and digging trenches in the fields on the edge of town. Wails from the wounded were muffled as they were buried alive in the mass grave.

Apparently, a few of the men in Kerala had been known to have fought with the *mujahiddin* ("freedom fighters") in the resistance movement against the Communists. The Russian-influenced government had wanted to use Kerala as an example and a warning to other communities with some ties to the resistance movement.

This story is only one of many tales of horror Betty and I heard spoken from the mouths of Afghan refugees when we traveled to Pakistan in the spring of 1980 as representatives of World Concern, a Seattle-based Christian relief agency. The widows and several thousand surviving children of Kerala had made their way on foot over the rugged mountain passes to the safety of Pakistan, just as approximately 1.5 million of their countrymen have since the spring of 1979.

All have left their homeland for the same reason. Rather than compromise their Islamic principles and submit to Communism, these people have supported the *jihad,* or "holy war" against the Russians. Most have left everything they own to escape the threat of death from a Russian bullet or poisonous gas. Their new home is usually one of approximately eighty crowded refugee camps dotting the Pakistan-Afghanistan border.

Our job was to assess refugee needs for food, clothing, and shelter so World Concern and other Christian relief agencies could better serve the needs of the people. While there, we learned of the role literally dozens of relief organizations were having in assisting displaced Afghans, including World Vision International, the World Relief Corporation, and the United Nations High Commission, to name only a few.

Betty and I had spent several days visiting a half-dozen different camps, talking with refugees in their native Dari or Pushtu languages. Survivors of the Kerala massacre are only a small percentage of over a million refugees living in Pakistan provinces northwest of Peshawar. No road led directly to the Kerala encampment, so we walked the final two miles through wheat and poppy fields to their settlement along a riverbank.

What we saw was repeated in almost every area we visited. Thousands of people were jammed together in a camp encompassing only a few square blocks. Disease and dysentery moved throughout the area like a plague. Children ran naked and played in the mud while the stench of rotting human excrement permeated the air. Most people lived in eight-by-sixteen-foot tents provided by the various relief agencies. However, there weren't enough to go around, and it was not uncommon for as many as five different families to share one tent. Those who didn't have tents were living in hastily built straw huts.

At Bajaur we visited the Pakistan official in charge of distributing money to refugees in several area camps. Each person was entitled to fifty Pakistani rupees a month—about sixteen cents a day. The head of each family signed for the money, and if he was illiterate, he placed his thumbprint next to his name.

Another two hundred thousand Afghan refugees were living in the area southwest of Peshawar near Kohat, Parachinar, and Bannu. Camps were structured so that people from the same town, village, and valley remained as a unit. Community spirit in Afghanistan is very strong, and it is not uncommon for a whole village to make their trek over the rugged terrain to Pakistan together. Most of the refugees have traveled by night to avoid detection by Russian jets and helicopter gunships on patrol.

One Afghan village wasn't so fortunate. Near Quetta in Waziristan province we learned of their sad fate. Unable to cross the Pakistan border because of a flash flood, daylight had found them unprotected in the Afghan desert. Soviet planes flew over and straffed these helpless refugees. Many men, women, and children died that morning with bullets in their backs.

The refugees by and large are appreciative of the food, shelter, and clothing provided by the relief effort, and they have adapted as well as can be expected to their meager existence. Many told us that the first ones to help them when they crossed the border were the Christians, especially from the Inter-Aid Committee of the Church of Pakistan. But ask them what they really want, and they'll answer immediately—"modern weapons."

The *mujahiddin* or "holy warriors" continue their fight with the Russians throughout the Afghan countryside against impossible odds. Unlike the Viet Cong in South Vietnam, the *mujahiddin* do not have the luxury of dense jungle cover and an unlimited supply of foreign-made munitions. Yet, using guerrilla tactics, their expert sniping ability, and their mobility by traveling at night over familiar terrain, the Afghan "freedom fighters" have been able to totally frustrate one hundred thousand of the best trained and equipped soldiers in the world.

The United States State Department estimated that Russian casualties one year after the invasion of December, 1979 had reached fifteen thousand. Military experts believe some two hundred and fifty thousand troops would be necessary before Russia could expect to have a firm grip on the entire country—an expensive proposition indeed!

Afghans feel like the rest of the world has abandoned them in their quest to oust the Russians from their homeland. The *mujahiddin* don't want anyone else to fight their war for them. They simply want a more sophisticated arsenal to combat the tanks, helicopter gunships, rockets, poisonous gas, and napalm used against them by the Russians.

But why have the Russians chosen to conquer Afghanistan, which has long been one of the more undeveloped third world nations? Approximately the size of Texas, the geography is primarily composed of barren desert and mountain wilderness. Some peaks tower as high as 24,000 feet and act as reservoirs, feeding streams and rivers that flow into the valleys and plains.

These mountain-fed waterways are the lifeblood of Afghanistan's 16 million people since rainfall in much of the country each year averages only ten inches.

Afghanistan contains little oil, and has few of the natural resources apart from natural gas and some minerals that the consuming nations of the West and Russia would covet. The vast majority of its citizens are poorly educated, and around three million are nomads. Like their ancestors before them, most Afghans are more than satisfied with the meager living they make from sheepherding, farming, or trading.

Why then has the iron claw of the Soviet machine unleashed its brutality on so innocent a victim? Why have the Soviets sent combat troops to the soil of a third world nation for the first time since their post World War II rise to power?

Throughout history, nonthreatening nations have been used time and time again as pawns in the military strategies of superpowers. The soldiers of Alexander the Great rolled over nation after nation as the Greeks spread their Hellenistic culture across most of the known ancient world. The armies of the Roman Empire, Charlemagne, Genghis Khan, Spain, Portugal, and more recently the Axis powers of Adolf Hitler's Germany and Tojo's Japan had no scruples about forcing their will on independent people—people living in nations that stood in the way of their quest for world supremacy.

Today, the leaders of the Soviet Union lust for world control. Afghanistan happens to have been in the wrong place at the wrong time.

Bordering oil-rich Iran on the west, and Pakistan on the south and east, Afghanistan's location will provide a strategic base for further expansion of Soviet power. Moscow radio vociferously denies it, but the Russian plan clearly is to use Afghanistan as a military base from which to attack the rest of Asia. Russian-built military airports in Afghanistan are close enough to allow the Soviets to eventually control shipping in the strategic Straight of Hormuz and the oil-rich Persian Gulf area. The southern boundary of Afghanistan lies only three hundred miles from the Indian Ocean. A quick invasion through the Pakistan province of Baluchistan would give the Soviet Union the warm water port they have sought for decades.

Russia long ago recognized Afghanistan's strategic value. So did the United States. Consequently, for the last three decades, Afghanistan has reaped the benefit of a foreign aid "tug-of-war." Soviet assistance to Afghanistan was heavily concentrated in the military realm before the invasion. It had been administered with future control of the country in mind. American aid, on the other hand, had been focused on helping Afghanistan with its educational development, and in assisting the Asian country to get on its feet economically.

The handwriting on the wall that foreshadowed the Soviet takeover may have started as long ago as 1953. That was the year United States Vice-president Richard Nixon made a diplomatic visit to Kabul. Desperately needing to upgrade its small, poorly equipped and trained army, the Afghan government requested American military assistance in the form of arms, heavy vehicles, and munitions. However, at that time, Afghanistan and Pakistan were feuding over territory in their border areas. Both sides claimed that a large area known as Pushtunistan, belonged to them.

Richard Nixon, President Eisenhower, and the State Department were caught in the horns of a dilemma. The cold war between East and West had reached its zenith, and the United States fully understood the importance of establishing friendly relations with this nation, which shares a nine-hundred-mile-long border with the Soviets.

But in those turbulent mid-fifties, war between Afghanistan and Pakistan appeared imminent. Since the United States was already supplying arms to Pakistan, the decision was made to deny Afghanistan's request for military hardware. The next year, 1954, the Afghan government began their flirtation with disaster. They turned to their disliked neighbors to the north for both military and economic assistance. This was the green light Russia was looking for, and the Soviets were more than happy to oblige.

Russian-made rifles, tanks, helicopters, and fighter planes soon made their way into the Afghan arsenal. The Russians also commensed a major highway building program to link the heart of Afghanistan with its new supplier to the north. Two different roadbeds—one running west and one south—were poured with concrete, reinforced with steel, to support tanks, trucks, and other heavy-duty military equipment.

The western road, heading southeast from the Russian border at Kushka, through Herat, and across the desert to Kandahar, carried hundreds of vehicles and over ten thousand troops to strategic points in southern and western Afghanistan during the first few days of the invasion in December, 1979. The second road winds its way south from the Soviet border at the Oxus River, through the towering Hindu Kush mountain range, and ends at Kabul. At one impass, over eleven thousand feet in elevation, the Russians blasted through two miles of solid rock. The tunnel is one of the longest and most expensive in the world. This highway is currently the major supply line for the Russian war effort in eastern Afghanistan combat zones.

American assistance sought to balance the Russian strategy by engineering highways that connect Afghanistan with Pakistan and Iran. For example, the highway from Kabul east through the Tangi Gharu Gorge to the Khyber Pass was built with American taxpayer money. United States engineers also paved an asphalt road from the capital to Kandahar and on south to the Pakistan border at Chaman. The United States can take the credit for the road from Herat in western Afghanistan to the Iranian border at Islam Qalah, as well.

But roadways were only part of the plan. The Soviets built several huge military airports in Afghanistan. The largest are at Bagram, forty miles north of Kabul, and Shindand in southwest Afghanistan. The United States concentrated on building civil airports to serve the people of several of Afghanistan's larger cities. Our country also assisted with the development of Afghanistan's national airline, Ariana.

In the late 1950s, a United Nations survey concluded that the mountain formations around Kabul would not permit a large and safe airport to be built near the city. The report recommended that the largest civilian airport should be built outside of Kandahar. Smaller planes would then shuttle passengers on the three hundred miles to Kabul.

For a few years, most foreign passengers checked through Afghan customs at the American-built Kandahar airport. Then the Russians went to work and literally moved the mountain, which blocked the approach to the Kabul airport. Kabul residents could hear dynamite blasts echoing in the distance for months. An estimated three hundred and fifty Soviet troop and cargo planes landed at the Kabul airport between December 24, 1979, and the December 27, 1979 coup. This would have been impossible had the approach never been cleared.

Other preparations were being made for the inevitable invasion. Several large fuel-storage tanks were built on the outskirts of Kabul. These are now supplying the gas tanks of Russian military vehicles. The Russians also constructed a bakery in Kabul in the late 1950s. Its silo is the tallest structure in the capital city. Many people laughed at how foolish the Russians appeared to be. The Afghan people bake their whole wheat bread fresh for every meal in their home floor ovens.

No one is laughing now. The bakery is in full production, manufacturing bread for Russian soldiers stationed throughout the country.

Other Russian aid included scholarships for Afghan army and air force officers to train in the Soviet Union. Many returned as Communists. Russia also sent students to attend Kabul University as propagandists for atheistic materialism. It wasn't long before a majority of the students in this institution became committed to the doctrines of Communism.

The 1950s and 1960s saw Mohammed Daoud as Afghanistan's prime minister. His major goal was to see Pushtunistan carved out of Pakistan, west of the Indus River, as an independent nation. An estimated 6 million people with Afghan roots live in this area. Pushtunistan would have included the port city of Karachi on the Indian Ocean. Daoud speculated that Pushtunistan would eventually unite with Afghanistan, giving the landlocked nation access to the sea. To accomplish all of this, Prime Minister Daoud sought even more military aid and equipment from his supplier—the Soviet Union.

Hostilities between Pakistan and Afghanistan reached their peak in the late 1950s and early 1960s. For several years, Pakistan closed its border with Afghanistan to trade and supplies. This meant that goods coming from Europe and America had to go through Russia or Iran, increasing Afghanistan's dependence on the Soviet Union. Afghanistan King Zahir Shah, prompted by his concern at the growing Russian presence in his country, forced the resignation of Prime Minister Daoud in 1963.

In July of 1973, Mohammed Daoud returned to power in a

Communist-backed coup that overthrew Afghanistan's monarchy. About one hundred men, most of whom were Russian-trained military officers helped put control of the country in Mohammed Daoud's hands literally overnight. Early in the morning Prime Minister Musa Shafiq was awakened and arrested in his pajamas. King Zahir Shah was out of the country at the time and is still in exile today.

Daoud declared the nation to be a republic and announced that he would serve as president, even though he had secretly joined the Communist Party. However, while in office, President Daoud became more and more disillusioned with the increasing domination of the Soviet Union. He traveled to several countries, including Saudi Arabia, in an effort to secure economic assistance to balance the Soviet influence.

In early April, 1978, an Afghan Communist leader was gunned down on a Kabul street, and the government was suspected of being behind the assassination. In a show of force, the Communists rallied thousands for the funeral. An aroused President Daoud arrested several of the Communist leaders, including the powerful Noor Mohammed Taraki, and put them in prison. Little did the Afghan leader realize that this was the excuse the Russian-backed Communists needed to stage a coup and overthrow his government.

It started on Thursday afternoon, April 27, 1978, and by evening the next day, the country was in Communist hands. President Daoud, members of his family, and several key leaders in his administration were murdered in cold blood in Kabul's Dil Kusha Palace. Noor Mohammed Taraki was released from prison and proclaimed head of the new regime.

Chaos inside Afghanistan was beginning to brew. The government claimed that its leaders were "Muslim Marxists." One banner headline in the government-controlled newspaper read: OUR GLORIOUS LEADERS UNSTINTINGLY SUPPORT THE HOLY ISLAMIC FAITH.

But in reality, the opposite was true. Most people realized that it was impossible to have "theist atheists." The Communists systematically began arresting Muslim leaders.

In prison, they were given the opportunity to join the Communist Party. If they refused, they were executed. If they agreed, initiation involved tearing and crumpling the pages of the Koran. All ties with their former Islamic faith were to be cut. Muslims retaliated by declaring a *jihad,* or "holy war" against the Communist government. Bitter fighting broke out in many rural areas around the country.

Meanwhile, President Taraki's corrupt administration was being torn by dissention. Another high official, Hafizullah Amin began to gain more and more support from within the party ranks. He had spent several years in the United States studying at Columbia Teachers College in New York City. Even though he was a confirmed Communist, he was determined that his country would not be taken over by Russia. The Soviet Union was suspicious of him and reportedly entered into a plot for President Taraki to assassinate him during a meeting.

However, someone tipped Amin off, and on September 19, 1979, he arrived at the meeting armed and shot the president first. Amin proclaimed himself to be the leader of the government and ordered the Soviet ambassador out of the country for the role he had played in the assassination plot.

President Amin promptly published a list of over fourteen thousand Afghans who had been executed during Taraki's seventeen months as head of state. Amin wanted the people to know how ruthless the previous government had been.

Russia was furious. Not only did the Soviets fear that Hafizullah Amin would steer Afghanistan away from their influence, Muslim freedom fighters were winning victory after victory against a Russian-controlled Afghan army. A military force of over one hundred thousand strong had been decimated to less than half that size by desertions. Thousands of Afghan soldiers refused to fight their own countrymen. Many defected to the *mujahiddin,* taking valuable Russian military equipment and munitions with them.

The *mujahiddin* controlled most of the Afghan countryside, and several of Afghanistan's major cities. Russian advisers doubted that the few remaining loyal troops could even defend Kabul from a "freedom fighter" attack.

Russian leaders knew invasion was the only way the Soviet Union could retain its grip on the Afghan political situation. They were faced with the decision either to withdraw completely or invade. And so with the attention of Western nations focused on the American hostages in Iran, the Soviets had the perfect cover for their unprecedented military maneuver.

Early on the frigid evening of December 27, 1979, Russian tanks rumbled through Kabul's snow-covered streets, while machine gun and rifle fire could be heard echoing into the cold night air. Russian infantry soldiers met rebel resistance at the Kabul radio station, but soon the guns of the small band of defenders were silenced. Just outside the southwestern city limits, a small battalion of Afghan soldiers loyal to President Hafizullah Amin were making a valiant stand at the Darulaman Palace. After a short skirmish, hundreds of Russian soldiers broke through the weak defenses and stormed into the residence. President Amin, his younger brother and nephew, and several government officials were captured and shot for "crimes against the people and the Afghan nation."

By morning, all was quiet throughout the capital city, except for the occasional buzzing of low-flying Russian jets and helicopters in the skies. Thousands of Kabul residents woke up to the sight of Russian soldiers patrolling their neighborhoods. People tuned into radio Afghanistan and listened to the words of the new president, Soviet-appointed Babrak Karmal. Karmal, an Afghan Communist and longtime friend of the Soviet Union, broadcasting from Russia, denounced the Amin dictatorship as an "agent of American imperialism." He then was flown into Kabul to assume the role of a Soviet puppet.

But through it all, the Russians made one serious mistake. They totally underestimated the will of the Afghan people to fight back. The Russian invasion only served to strengthen the people's resolve to oust the atheistic foreigners from their land.

Military experts have been baffled by the incredible courage the ill-equipped *mujahiddin* have shown in the face of impossible odds—a courage spawned by an intense devotion to the pillars of their Islamic faith. Consequently, a basic understanding of Islam is essential to anyone who desires to comprehend the iron will of the Afghan people—an iron will that has not been broken by the iron claw of the Soviet war machine.

3
The Country of the Afghan

"Drop by drop a river is made." [*qatra qatra daryaw maisha (wad)*.]
Afghan proverb

Afghanistan means "the country (istan) of the Afghan." Approximately half of Afghanistan's 16 million population belong to the Afghan tribes (also known as the Pushtuns or Pathan tribe), and these people are concentrated in the eastern and southern portions of the country.

Afghanistan's second largest ethnic group are the Tadjiks who are of Persian background. Approximately 3 million strong, the Tadjiks are primarily tenant farmers and laborers scattered throughout northern and western Afghanistan.

The land between the Soviet border in the far north and the Hindu Kush mountain range in northcentral Afghanistan is home for about eight hundred thousand Uzbeks who are related to the people across the northern border in Soviet Uzbekistan. The Turkomen, of Turkish ancestry, are a group of about two hundred thousand pastoral nomads found mostly near Iran and Russia in the northwest.

Hazarajat is in central Afghanistan named for the approximately six hundred thousand Hazaras whose ancestral roots date back seven hundred and fifty years to the invading army of

Genghis Khan. These people are distinctly Mongolian in their appearance. North and west of the Hazaras live a people called the Chamar-Aimak and the mountains of northeast Afghanistan are home for about one hundred thousand Nuristanis. These village-dwelling mountain people are characterized by blond hair and blue eyes, which has made some anthropologists believe they are related to the Scandanavians through ancient migrations.

In all, fifty-two different languages are spoken within Afghanistan's borders, and the people are deeply divided by diverse tribal ways and customs. Yet, the Afghan nation has been united by one powerful force—their faith in Allah. Almost all Afghans are Muslims, bound together by the legal code of Islamic law. Islam is more than just a faith. It is a way of life. To begin to understand the complex makeup of the Muslim mindset, one must have a basic understanding of what Muslim people believe.

Islam is based on the teachings of the prophet Mohammed, as spelled out in the Koran. This Islamic holy book plus the traditions (*hadith*) detail how a Muslim should conduct his prayers, his business, his marriage, his wars—the whole spectrum of his life. Born in Mecca about 570 A.D., Mohammed wrote the Koran between 610 and his death in 632, based upon his religious knowledge and several "visions" which he describes.

Though Mohammed was influenced greatly by Judaism and Christianity, the tragedy was that none of the Scriptures had as yet been translated into Arabic, the only language he knew. Mohammed had to depend on oral sources and traditions for his knowledge of the Bible. Consequently, the Koran includes a distorted version of who Jesus Christ is.

The Koran describes Jesus' virgin birth, and miracles such as healing the sick and raising the dead. It states that Jesus was a great prophet who lived a sinless life. The Koran also describes Christ's ascension into Heaven. And Muslims believe in the second coming of Jesus. However, Islam is a heresy of Christianity because the Koran denies the deity of Christ.

Mohammed misunderstood the Trinity. He saw a decadent form of Christianity in Arabia where people worshiped pictures and statues of Mary. He concluded that Christians worshiped a holy family of God the Father, Mary the mother, and Jesus the Son. Consequently, the Koran affirms over and over again that God is one and repeatedly denies that God can have a Son. It is very difficult for a Muslim to understand how God has also revealed himself in his Son, Jesus Christ, and in the Holy Spirit.

Most Muslims not only deny the deity of Christ, but also his death. Certain verses in the Koran seem to indicate that Jesus did indeed die, but others seem to state otherwise. Muslim theologians, however, have usually interpreted the Koran to say that Jesus was too good a man to die on the cross. They claim that God caused the likeness of Jesus to fall on Judas who then was arrested and killed; whereas Jesus was taken up to heaven before the crucifixion. By rejecting Christ's death, Muslims disavow the sacrifice of Jesus on the cross for the sins of the world—the heart of the Christian gospel.

There are numerous factors contributing to the strong loyalty Muslims have for their faith. First, one must understand that Islam teaches salvation by works. Muslims have several religious duties that they must perform in order to be considered spiritual people. These duties are often referred to as the "six pillars of Islam."

Pillar one: "There is no God but Allah, and Mohammed is the apostle of Allah."

Muslims believe that anyone who confesses this creed becomes a member of their religion. They are supposed to repeat this word of witness over and over again, and some do it millions of times throughout their lives.

Pillar two: Prayer.

Five times each day, Muslims all over the world face Mecca and go through various genuflections while repeating the first chapter of the Koran in Arabic. Early in the morning, at noon, in the midafternoon, at sunset, and in the evening, one can hear the call to prayer from the minarets in cities, towns, and villages all over the Muslim world. Worshipers are supposed to go through ablutions of washing their feet, arms, and head prior to saying their prayers.

Pillar three: Giving alms.

Donating to the poor is required for salvation. Those who receive such gifts often feel they are doing the giver a favor, since they are providing the means for his or her salvation.

Pillar four: Fasting.

One lunar month each year, Muslims fast. In Afghanistan, this time is called *Ramazan*. The fast extends each day from the first light of dawn in the morning and continues to sunset. Nothing including food, drink, or even smoke, is allowed to pass the person's lips.

The fast has the effect of bringing about a religious revival since Muslims spend extra time praying and reading the Koran. People are allowed to eat and drink at night to prepare for the next day.

Pillar five: Pilgrimage to Mecca.

A person is encouraged to travel to the sacred sites in and around Mecca once during his or her lifetime. Airlines all over the Muslim world have profited by taking Muslim pilgrims to Saudi Arabia. The pilgrimage takes place once a year in commemoration of Abraham's attempted sacrifice of his son, who Muslims believe was Ishmael, rather than Isaac. Once a person has been to Mecca, the honorific title of *hajji* is given.

Pillar six: *Jihad,* or holy war.

Muslims believe that fighting for their faith assists them with their salvation. Should they die in battle, they believe their entrance into Heaven is assured. This accounts for the readiness of many Afghans to die fighting the Russians.

Besides the "six pillars of Islam," there are other pressures designed to keep Muslims true to their religion. Under the Islamic system of law, apostasy is punishable by death.

Islam is viewed much like a physical body. Therefore, if a limb is cut off, it hurts the whole community. Family honor is deeply bruised if a relative leaves the Muslim faith. In fact, Christian converts in Afghanistan on occasion have been murdered by their own relatives.

Muslim religious leaders teach that if an apostate is killed, he will still go to Heaven because of the blood he has shed for his sin. The person doing the killing is also assured of his salvation.

Before Afghan laws began to be secularized under Presidents Daoud, Taraki, Amin, and Karmal, judges who decided legal matters were Muslim *mullahs*. One of their functions was to convict and execute apostates.

This strong loyalty to the tenets of Islam has made the Afghan people, as well as other Muslim peoples in central and western

Asia, such as the Iranians, xenophobic not only toward the Communists, but toward the "Christian" West as well. Any non-Muslim is automatically viewed with suspicion.

Christians have had to contend with the same deep-seated religious hatred that has greeted the Communist atheists. Subsequently, this attitude has made Afghanistan one of the world's most closed nations to Christ's gospel. For many Christians, just getting into Afghanistan has been a miracle in itself, as you will see before finishing this book.

I know I'll never forget a hot June afternoon thirty years ago. That was when I received the final OK allowing me to go to "the country of the Afghan."

4
For Better or Worse

"Let Christians practice their own religion, and let Jews practice theirs." [*isaw ba deeni khud, a moosaw ba deeni khud.*]

Afghan proverb

It was early Friday afternoon, June 22, 1951. My passport still had not arrived, and I was scheduled to leave New York for Afghanistan the following Monday. I had spent four years waiting to be sent to Afghanistan. Nothing would keep me off that plane. Not wanting to imagine any difficulty, I reasoned that the document had been mailed to the wrong address. So I wandered into the United States Passport Division office at the State Department to inquire as to its whereabouts.

It didn't take me long to realize that the passport had not been lost in the mail. After a "runaround" from office to office, I found myself standing in front of the large desk of D. S., director of the United States Passport Division. The State Department had no intention of issuing my passport. . . .

As I stood there waiting I thought how long I had been preparing for this opportunity. Actually the pieces had begun to fit together from the time I was born. I had spent the first fourteen years of my life as the son of missionaries in Iran, learning the ways of the Muslim people. In 1936, I had boarded a ship to the United States to commence my high school education at New Jersey's Lawrenceville Prep School, and four years later I enrolled at nearby Princeton University.

During World War II, I had enlisted in the army reserve but was discharged to prepare for the chaplaincy. While studying at Princeton Theological Seminary, I had worked on weekends as a staff member, and then as missionary secretary, for the Inter-Varsity Christian Fellowship (IVCF). When World War II ended, I accepted a position as full-time missionary secretary with Inter-Varsity, shortly after their merger with the Student Foreign Missions Fellowship. In this capacity I had directed the first Inter-Varsity student missions conference held in Toronto in 1946 (now known as Urbana).

It was there that I met my future wife, Betty Hutton, then a Canadian kindergarten teacher. She had asked me to arrange an interview with Dr. Samuel Zwemer, a former missionary pioneer to the Muslim world. She had an interest in teaching Islamic children, and I figured that anyone who wanted to work with Muslims had to be special.

It was in February of 1947 when I first heard of a need for teachers in Afghanistan. Soon I was sure the Lord wanted me to go there. I filled out the necessary forms and submitted my application. Thinking the way to Afghanistan would soon open, I informed Inter-Varsity I would be resigning from my position with them that summer. However, months passed and I didn't hear anything. So I made temporary alternate plans to study in Edinburgh, Scotland, that fall in order to better prepare myself for work in a Muslim area.

The very day I sailed from New York, a letter came to my home inviting me to come to Washington, D.C., for an interview. The letter was forwarded to me in Scotland. I answered that I was now working on a doctorate but would be more than willing to interrupt my studies if they wanted me to go to Afghanistan.

The reply stated: "There is no need for you to return to the States for an interview. We have had enough applicants. . . . Continue your studies and reapply after you have earned your degree."

Naturally, I was disappointed, but that delay turned out to be a blessing. My dissertation focused on Mohammed's prophetic office as portrayed in the Koran. The knowledge I obtained during my studies came in very handy through the twenty-two years I finally had the opportunity to share the gospel with Afghan Muslims in Afghanistan.

I returned to the United States from Scotland in the summer of 1949 and met with Dick Soderberg, who was at that time recruiting faculty for a new school, the Afghan Institute of Technology (see chapter 12). He asked if I would be willing to head up the English Department. I agreed. While waiting to go, I took courses in linguistics and teaching English as a second language at Columbia Teachers College in New York City.

Betty and I were married in June, 1950, fully anticipating that we would shortly leave for Afghanistan. We had become increasingly concerned as time passed without the final OK. Then, early in the winter of 1951, a letter arrived from Dick. It seemed that an American family in Afghanistan knew that my parents had been missionaries in Iran. They had spread a rumor that I was probably going to Afghanistan to be a Christian missionary. This, of course, was unacceptable to the Afghan Muslims. It would be unwise to jeopardize the whole AIT project by bringing us on board at that time. "You better wait for three to five more years until the matter is forgotten," Dick had written.

Needless to say, Betty and I were disappointed. It had now been four years since I had made my first application to teach in Afghanistan. But God renewed our call and encouraged us with a promise from Numbers 14: 8: "If the Lord is pleased with us, then he will bring us into this land, and give it to us. . . . " If we were faithful in obeying the Lord and following his leading, he would open the way before us.

With renewed peace, I went to work as an associate to Dr. Herbert Mekeel, pastor at the First Presbyterian Church in Schenectady, New York. Again, God used the additional delay to prepare us for his work in Afghanistan. As we waited we grew in the pastoral experience we would later need. And we got to know praying people who stood behind our vision of reaching Afghanistan with the true message of Christ.

Although we did not know it, God was already at work answering our prayers. In March, 1951, the "apostle to the illiterates," Dr. Frank Laubach, and his literacy team finished an Afghanistan project. Dr. Laubach had been invited by the

Afghan Ministry of Education to write the curriculum for reading courses in Afghanistan's Dari and Pushtu languages (see chapter 12). Dr. Laubach's team included my father, J. Christy Wilson, who served as an interpreter.

At the literacy team's farewell reception conducted by the Afghan government, His Excellency, Dr. Abdul Majid, the minister of education, asked Dr. Laubach if he knew of any other English teachers who could come to Afghanistan. Doctor Laubach told him to speak with my father who was a team member and he gave Dr. Majid my address. Through Howard Larsen, the American principal of Habibia High School, I received a cable from the Afghan Ministry of Education offering me an English teaching position at the oldest secondary school in the country.

Betty and I were overwhelmed by the ways of God. After four years of red tape and frustration, my hands held a personal invitation from the top Afghanistan education official.

My father, after his return from Afghanistan, had accompanied me to Washington to speak with the acting Afghan ambassador. I felt it only right that he know I was a Christian minister before I signed my contract. I wanted to make sure he, or other Afghan officials, would not later feel I had signed under false pretenses.

This, the ambassador told me, was not a problem. "Most Afghan teachers are Muslim *mullahs* (priests)," he had said. "It will be good to have a Christian priest teaching our young people."

I also mentioned a clause in the contract, which concerned me. It stated that I agreed "not to interfere in business, politics, and/or religion." I had asked His Excellency just what this meant. "If a student asks me a religious question, does this mean that I am not free to answer him?"

He replied, "By no means. If a student asks you a question, as a teacher, you have an obligation to answer.

"This clause," he continued, "was put in the contracts in order to prevent anyone from raising a religious riot."

He went on to explain the reason for such a clause. Representatives of the heretical Muslim Ahmadiyya or Qardiani Sect had preached their doctrines in the streets of Afghanistan and caused riots in the 1940s.

I thanked him for his clarification and signed the contract. My father, who was with me as a witness, wrote a paper documenting the conversation in case it might be needed for future reference.

I should have known there was going to be trouble when four days before our scheduled flight to Afghanistan I received a person-to-person phone call from the Afghanistan embassy in Washington. I was asked to come back again and see officials there the next day. "We are not sure you are going after all!" the Afghan secretary on the other end of the line concluded.

I asked him the reason, since the contract had already been signed and authorized. He said he could not discuss it on the telephone. I would have to see the acting ambassador again in person. That night we ran up quite a phone bill urging friends to make my trip to Washington the next day a matter of prayer.

And their prayers surrounded me the next day as I talked to the Afghan ambassador in his office. He said that he wanted to make sure I understood the religious situation in his nation. I responded that since I had grown up in Iran, I was quite familiar with Muslim people. I mentioned that my desire was to help his nation and his people. I had no intention of causing any trouble.

He was convinced of my sincerity and assured me that he was happy I was going to work among his people. He served me tea, and asked if I wouldn't mind doing him a favor. He walked out of the room and returned with a half dozen new Arrow shirts he wanted to give to the prime minister in Kabul.

But I still hadn't received my passport which was why I now stood in D.S.'s fancy office. I had been cleared by the Afghanistan government, but representatives of my own country still had questions.

"What is your primary purpose for going to Afghanistan?" the director interrogated. "Do you intend to preach the gospel?"

I answered as honestly as I knew how. "I know Afghanistan does not have religious freedom, but I believe God is going to open that land. When he does, I will count it a privilege to witness for my Lord."

"That is what we were afraid of!" D. S. huffed. "By the way, what has the Afghan embassy said about your going?"

I referred to my two conversations with the Afghan ambassador and mentioned that I had just come from tea in his office.

D. S. knew she had no legal grounds to deny my passport application. United States law states that international travel privileges can only be denied to those in favor of the forcible overthrow of American government.

The passport director proceeded to send me from State Department office to State Department office—in one final effort to dissuade me. After a while, I began to think I was listening to a broken record. Every official had the same message. It would be foolish for a Protestant minister to live in religiously sensitive Afghanistan located on the Russian and Chinese borders. Muslims had long resisted any Christian influence, which I knew, and still objected to any religious presence other than Islam.

But I knew God had called me to serve there; I had watched him perform several miracles to get me this far. I wasn't about to listen to the advice I was getting from the Washington bureaucrats. Reluctantly, the State Department finally approved my passport—just before they closed for the weekend.

The thermometer rested at 115 degrees when Betty and I checked into Dean's Hotel in Peshawar, Pakistan, two weeks later. Afghanistan still had no available plane service, so we had arrived in the dust-choked city, not knowing how we would travel the final 180 miles over the Khyber Pass and on to Kabul. The only public passenger transportation (a converted truck) made the journey over the rough mountain roads only twice a week. With Betty five months pregnant, I decided a ride in the back end of a truck would be too risky. We asked about renting a taxi, but discovered that the Peshawar-to-Kabul run was not very popular. Two hundred dollars was a bit more than I could afford. Committing the matter to prayer, we sat back and watched God perform yet another miracle.

That evening as Betty and I were forcing down a greasy curry dinner in the hotel dining room, a man sporting a thick British accent walked up to our table.

"Doctor and Mrs. Wilson, I want to welcome you to Afghanistan. Tomorrow morning, our chauffeur will be waiting to drive you to Kabul."

Just as suddenly, the man was gone. Betty and I looked at each other in stunned silence. The hotel manager later explained that the Britisher was with the United Nations and was returning to England. The manager had assumed we also were with the United Nations. When the UN expert was looking for a couple he was to meet at the hotel, the manager had pointed us out to him.

That night, I went to the man's room and explained the mistake. He was surprised, but said if we could find the couple he was looking for, we were more than welcome to ride along with them.

We all loaded into the Chevrolet station wagon shortly after dawn the next morning. But the roads were so poor that it was almost midnight before we reached Kabul. In 1951 Kabul was far from the tourist capital of the world, and the hotel was already closed. The chauffeur banged on the door and eventually a sleepy-eyed manager showed us to a dingy room.

Blood marks stained the bed sheets where the former occupants had obviously killed mosquitoes. There was a high incidence of malaria in the city, and, at that time, approximately half of those who came to Afghanistan contracted the disease.

"We can't stay here," Betty said to me. "We must go to another hotel!"

I thought of our marriage vows—"for better or worse"—when I replied, "This is the only one there is."

However, it wasn't long before we were able to rent a place of our own, and I began my teaching duties at Habibia. Betty was kept plenty busy being mother to our daughter Nancy.

The early 1950s saw real growth in Kabul's international community. Since I was the only ordained Protestant minister in Afghanistan, my services were constantly in demand. In addition to my school responsibilities, I preached in services held in homes, and also conducted several weddings and funerals. In December, 1952, I was asked to pastor the newly organized Community Christian Church—a job I was to fill for the next two decades. Members primarily included foreign diplomats, engineers, and teachers living in Kabul.

Services were held weekly through mid-1953 in the home of American Ambassador Angus Ward. But as the congregation grew, we had to rent a house with a large room in the *Karte Char* district of the city (Kabul's southwestern section). This was to become our home for several years.

I had become grateful for a clause in my teaching contract which stated that I would be given my own holy days off. Most people in the non-Muslim international community went ahead and worked Sundays to conform to the Afghan culture. (Friday is the Muslim holy day.)

But I had felt led that I be freed from my teaching responsibilities on Sunday. Minister of Education Abdul Majid had given me permission if I would accept a one-sixth cut in my salary. This gave me time to preach and have Sunday school classes in our home for the international community children. However, as my church responsibilities grew, it became obvious that I could no longer do justice to both jobs. I was trying "to carry two watermelons in one hand," as an Afghan saying goes.

Howard Larsen, by then the acting resident representative for the United Nations, explained my dilemma to the Afghan government. He requested that permission be granted to allow me to become full-time chaplain to the international community. The Italian embassy housed a Roman Catholic priest, and since there were more Protestants than Catholics in Afghanistan, it seemed reasonable that I be given a visa for such a position. His Excellency Abdul Rahman Pajwak, who had been president of the United Nations General Assembly in New York, graciously sent a letter from the Afghan government, granting this permission.

But the decision still was not an easy one. Columbia Teachers College of New York had just signed a contract with the Afghan government to supply teachers for, and administrate Afghanistan's educational system. The Teachers College offered me an advisory role and a job as director of English teaching.

The benefits over what I had been receiving as a member of the Habibia faculty were great. Under most circumstances, duty-free privileges and a triple increase in salary would be hard to turn down. Especially, when the chaplaincy meant depending on the goodwill of our parishioners for support. We had no idea what our eventual salary with the church was going to be. But then, a board of trustees for the Kabul Community Christian Church was established in the States to help with special projects and our partial support.

In the end, however, God led Betty and me to realize there

was no decision to make. My job was to serve the international community—a task I performed until 1973 as pastor of the Kabul Community Christian Church. Those years turned out to be the most rewarding and fulfilling period of my life. Not only did the church provide spiritual fellowship and growth for many in the international community, several outreach ministries had a profound impact on the Afghan nationals as well.

5
The Way Out

"I have never seen one go astray who traveled along the right highway." [*kas nadeedam ki kaj shud az rawe rawst.*]

Afghan Proverb

Most Muslims view themselves as spiritual, and brand those from the "Christian" West as secular materialists. Anti-American and anti-Western sentiment runs very deep in Afghanistan.

I can't say that I blame the Afghans for feeling the way they do. The conservative Islamic culture is a highly moral one. The Afghans have been shocked by what they have considered to be "pagan" values exhibited by many Westerners traveling and living in their country.

Much of the antagonism has come from the dichotomy of life-styles, particularly the difference between those who are committed to some faith, as the Muslims are, and those who have little religious belief at all.

Pornography in the form of X-rated films horrified the Afghans once such films were admitted into the country. Traditional Sunni Islam has a prohibition against any picture as a form of idolatry. To show movies was bad enough, but to depict "erotic sensuality" was beyond forgiveness.

Many members of the international community in Afghanistan also engaged in immorality. Afghans quickly concluded that Westerners lived just the way the pornographic films depicted life. Numerous cocktail parties in the foreign diplomatic and business circles further insulted the Afghan culture, whose Islamic religion prohibits the drinking of wine and liquor.

I once knew a heavy drinking American in Kabul who was shocked when his Muslim neighbor informed him that he had become a Christian.

"What do you mean you've become a Christian?" the American said.

The Afghan answered, "I drink whiskey now like you do. Do you have any you can give me?"

To him, becoming a Christian meant leaving the prohibition of Islam against the use of alcohol and indulging like his neighbor.

Even the Western fashions, miniskirts and sleeveless blouses, were exhibitions of nudity to the Muslim mind. Some Muslim *mullahs* would throw acid on the legs of Afghan girls who dressed in the Western short skirts.

Other factors have played a part in developing the Afghans' disillusionment toward so-called "Christian" countries. The past three decades have seen a great many Afghan citizens travel to Western nations. Often they were not received with the same kindness they offered outsiders to their own country. Afghans look on hospitality as an important courtesy. Many times Betty and I felt like we were treated like royalty when we were being entertained by an Afghan family.

Many Afghan travelers were disillusioned when they were not received into Western homes the same way, and often they felt lonely and rejected. Communist organizations around the world took full advantage of this and went out of their way to befriend Afghan international students and visitors. Many returned to Afghanistan as ardent Marxists. They formed an important base for the Communist coup that took over the country in April of 1978.

Tourists set the poorest example of Western life. Afghanistan's doors were opened to tourists for the first time in 1957. The number of travelers grew until as many as one hundred thousand people a year visited the country. Thousands of Western young people arrived and were walking the streets of Kabul and other cities. Many were experimenting with drugs and studying Eastern religions. The local people were stunned by the number who were anxious to get hard drugs, produced from opium poppies, a popular Afghan crop. Hundreds were caught smuggling drugs and Afghan prisons were soon overflowing with foreigners. Many young people died of overdoses, and others lost their minds. Moreover, many of the women would engage in prostitution to get money to satisfy expensive drug habits.

Desperate and disillusioned, some of these young people began to seek for further meaning in life. We at the Kabul Community Christian Church sensed a wide open opportunity to help young people get their lives back together. And so began a saga that ended with one of the most unusual ministries I've ever had the privilege to be a part of.

First, members of our church contacted the Salvation Army headquarters in New York about establishing a center in Kabul to care for these young people. They expressed an interest, but Afghan officials would not allow people wearing the Salvation Army uniform to work in their nation.

We also wrote to David Wilkerson of Teen Challenge, but this organization did not feel it could expand its ministry to Afghanistan.

Jim Cameron, from New Zealand, came through Kabul and told our church about Youth with a Mission, an organization committed to training young people for evangelism. In July of 1970 Youth with a Mission staff members Jim and Jan Rogers arrived in Kabul with seven dedicated young people. They stayed in the Nuristan Hotel, a disreputable hangout for world travelers. The atmosphere in that "flop house" was vile and the hotel reeked of hashish and opium smoke. Immorality was rampant. The group did their best to minister to these lost young people, but little spiritual progress was made that first summer.

The following June, a team of fifteen Youth with a Mission workers drove to Kabul from Europe. Much had been learned from the previous summer's experience and so our church rented two top floors of a center city hotel. In a few days the team began a dining room-tea room ministry called, "The Way Out."

The rules of behavior were very strict. Young people climbing the ninety-two stairs to the roof restaurant read the regulations at the entrance: "No smoking of anything. No immorality or bad language allowed. Any who do not abide by these regulations will have to leave."

God answered prayer and many young people became Christians through The Way Out ministry. The young people of The Way Out also began visiting local prisons. Through their witness God began moving among drug addicts and smugglers imprisoned there.

One German boy had been put in prison because the Afghan police found him wandering aimlessly about the Kabul streets. He did not know his name or nationality but the police located his passport in his pocket. Although his family had offered to pay his way back to Germany, no airline would accept the responsibility of taking him unless a doctor or nurse was in attendance. So The Way Out young people asked permission to take him to their residence, which the police readily granted, happy to get rid of him.

The young man was terribly undernourished, so he was fed with good, nutritious food. He had become demon-possessed during involvement with Eastern religions and evil spirits forced him to try to commit suicide. He once slit his wrists, and another time tried to jump off the hotel's sixth floor onto the pavement below.

A Christian young person had to be with him all the time, watching him and praying for him. Finally, he came to his senses and he was led to a personal faith in Jesus Christ. Day by day, you could see a tremendous transformation taking place in his life.

The next time the Afghan police saw him, they refused to believe that he was the same person until they checked his passport. They asked what had happened, which gave him the opportunity to share the power that comes from repentance and receiving Jesus as Savior. "If any man be in Christ, he is a new creation," he told them.

Officials in the German embassy were utterly amazed when he walked into their offices, healed and in his right mind. When he told them about The Way Out, they sent a representative to investigate. As he went through the two floors, meeting converts who a short time before had been on heavy drugs, and whose faces now showed the light of their newfound joy, he said, "Wunderbar! I never imagined that anything like this was possible. Why wasn't The Way Out started in Kabul long before this?"

He returned and gave a full report to the German Embassy, and a voluntary offering was received from the members of the staff to assist with the ministry.

That same summer, another Youth with a Mission team headed up by Floyd and Sally McClung witnessed as they traveled "the hippie trail" between Europe and Nepal. As they came back through Afghanistan in late August, five of their team felt called to stay and continue the Kabul ministry. Realizing the need for a place where converts could be isolated from their former associates in the drug culture, a house was rented in a Kabul suburb. The new place was called *Dilaram* (heart's peace). The McClungs kept in close touch with our church, and thirty or forty of these young people attended the services every Sunday.

I will never forget a service in January, 1973, when eight young men and women from *Dilaram* were baptized in one service. There was hardly a dry eye in the church as they shared their incredible testimonies. One Afghan young man in attendance said, "I saw the light of God on their faces."

The Youth with a Mission ministry in Kabul grew to the point that new converts, along with mature Christian young people, were sent to establish similar work in Kathmandu, Nepal, and New Delhi, India. A headquarters for the Dilaram ministry was also established in Amsterdam as well as a farm in the Dutch countryside.

The Way Out had helped many Afghanistan visitors escape the evil clutches of the drug culture and find new lives in Christ. But not every tourist who entered Afghanistan was a bad example to the Afghan people. Far from it. One American tourist is almost single-handedly responsible for starting an education program for Afghanistan's blind—a program which is still operating today with Russian blessing.

6
"Sight" for the Blind

"Hearing is never as good as seeing." [*shooneeda (n) kai boowad mawnindi deeda (n).*]

Afghan proverb

"We must do something for this little boy. He is without hope."

So were the concerned words of Afghanistan visitor Johnny Morris when he brought nine-year-old blind Mohdullah to our home in 1959. Johnny had grown up as an orphan in Savannah, Georgia, which gave him real empathy for the Afghan boy.

Johnny and I took Mohdullah to a doctor to have his eyes examined and learned he was incurably blind. Nothing medically could be done for him.

Johnny had taken a special interest in Mohdullah's future and was disappointed to learn that the Afghan Ministry of Education had no plans for rehabilitation of the blind. At that time in Afghanistan, all Mohdullah could look forward to was a mosque school where he would learn to memorize the entire Koran. That way he could recite it for pay at funerals, weddings, and other functions.

That prospect was not satisfactory to Johnny Morris who was looking for a constructive way to share the fortune he had inherited from his parents. So Johnny made an offer to the Afghan Ministry of Education: He would pay for a school building for the blind, for furnishings, and for teachers for one year, if the Ministry would agree to take over operational responsibility after that first year.

The Afghan Cabinet members were impressed that a person from another country was concerned about their blind. However, they felt they could not spare teachers or money for a school for the blind. The reason? Many sighted children in the country still did not have an opportunity for schooling.

Before Johnny Morris left Afghanistan, he bought Mohdullah a flute, and left a small scholarship for his support. Johnny did not want the money to be given directly to him, and so he stipulated that the money be used as reimbursement for odd jobs that Mohdullah would do. Each week Mohdullah came to the home we rented for the church with his smaller sighted sister leading him. Once there he did odd jobs, like pulling dandelions out of the lawn in the church garden. It was easy for him to feel the difference between the choking weeds and blades of grass.

About this time we had a visit from Dr. Isobel Grant, who herself was completely blind. She was working under a Fulbright grant, traveling to various countries to help with the education of the blind. She encouraged my wife, Betty, to teach Mohdullah to read and write Dari Braille. Betty said yes thinking the lessons would only take a couple of hours a week. Little did she realize that teaching the blind would soon be her full-time occupation.

When the lessons began, Mohdullah told Betty about two other blind friends who wanted to "read with their fingers." The three boys soon went through the whole first reader of the Afghan educational system. The primer had been typed in Dari Braille by Hans Werner, a Christian construction worker from Germany, who had been trained in the education of the blind and helped in his spare time.

Then in November of 1965 the prayers of Johnny Morris and many others were finally answered. His Excellency Dr. Mohammed Anas, the Afghan minister of education, accepted an invitation for tea in our home. First, we showed him the movie, *The Miracle Worker,* the story of Helen Keller. Then Dr. Anas met the three blind boys who read to him from the first primer. He apparently had never seen Braille read before, nor did he realize that there was a Dari system for it.

At first he thought the boys had memorized everything. But

when he selected several different parts of the book, he suddenly realized that the boys *were* reading.

"This is magic!" he exclaimed. In fact, he was so thrilled that he invited the blind boys, along with the Afghan girl who was helping, to come to his office at the Ministry the next day. There he gave them presents, and offered the Afghan girl a scholarship to go abroad and study work with the blind. He also announced over the radio and in the newspapers that any blind person who wanted to learn Braille and handicrafts should come to our home. The advertising worked and it wasn't long before we were swamped with more than seventy blind students.

Betty had to give up her teaching at the Christian school, Ahlman Academy (see chapter 12), in order to meet this new opportunity. Several church members volunteered to help out and another outreach of the Kabul Community Christian Church was under way. Pastor Sigfried Wiesinger, the director of the Christoffel Blindenmission in Germany, was invited to come to Afghanistan to give much needed advice in this emergency. His assistance proved invaluable in those first hectic months.

The Lord filled personnel needs in other ways. We received a letter just at that time from Kathleen Stewart, who was a fully trained teacher of the blind. She was wondering if her talents could be put to use somewhere in Afghanistan.

"Yes," we answered gladly, and she soon arrived under the International Afghan Mission (see chapter 14), sponsored by The Evangelical Alliance Mission.

A property was rented for the new school, next door to where the church was meeting, and the school was dedicated with the name—the Blind Institute of Noor in Afghanistan (BINA), which in Dari means "sight."

Other skilled teachers were secured from abroad, and local Afghans were trained. Eventually the first six years of the Afghan Ministry of Education curriculum were offered in Dari Braille. Handicrafts also were taught, as well as English. Students who desired to do so were then able to go on with their education in the sighted schools. Those who preferred to continue with handicrafts did so in their homes. At first the pupils were all boys, but after several years blind girls and tiny children started coming as well.

Other teachers of the blind found their way into Afghanistan.

Liisa Jakkula came from Finland to work and was later joined by her fiance, Ben Kingma, from the Netherlands. They were married in Kabul, and all the blind students and their families were invited to the Christian wedding, which was followed by a big feast of rice—an Afghan custom.

Theo and Ilse Reusch came from Germany to take over the Institute's administrative duties.

Finding the space to accommodate the young people attending the school was always a problem. The rented house next door was overflowing with blind children every day. The decision was made to build on the same property which was to house Kabul's new Eye Institute (see chapter 13).

Oxford Famine Relief (OXFAM), a British relief agency, gave money for the construction. Unfortunately, the building was not used for its intended purpose until nine years after its completion in 1970. At that time, the Afghan Ministry of Public Health insisted that the new BINA building be used as a temporary eye hospital until the main ophthalmological unit next door could be built.

Then, in March 1973 the unthinkable happened. The reactionary Muslim government under Prime Minister Musa Shafiq banned the Blind Institute from operating. Foreign teachers were ordered to leave Afghanistan within one week and some students who had studied in the Institute went back to begging on the streets.

Mohammed Shafiq had implemented a purge of non-Muslim sponsored activity throughout Afghanistan. The Blind Institute was especially vulnerable since some of the blind who had attended became Christians.

However, our great disappointment has now turned to joy. In 1979 the Communist regime reopened the blind school under the direction of a former BINA graduate. This was the fulfillment of a promise the Lord had given us in 1970: "And I will lead the blind by a way they do not know, in paths they do not know I will guide them. I will make darkness into light before them and rugged places into plains. These are the things I will do, and I will not leave them undone." (Isaiah 42: 16)

Today, for the first time, the Institute occupies the building which was constructed for that very purpose over a decade ago.

7
Spreading the Word

"A trumpeter's job is to blow." [*surnaicheer-a(-aw) chees(t) puf.*]
Afghan proverb

Marty, our four-year-old, asked me one evening as I was praying with him and putting him to bed, "Daddy, does Santa Claus
come to Afghan homes too?" It had dawned on him that
Christmas in Afghanistan was only celebrated in the international community.

That simple little question spawned what, from 1962 to 1980,
became an annual tradition at the Kabul Community Christian
Church. Each Christmas we produced an outdoor pageant
which would rival any performed in the States. We taped
appropriate sound effects, and spotlights lit up the scenes as the
actors reverently presented the Christmas story at night under
the stars. Donkeys, camels, sheep—we used them all. Needless
to say, we always seemed to arouse the curiosity of the local
Afghans.

Each year, despite their government's anti-Christian attitude,
more and more Afghans attended our pageant and heard the
good news of Jesus' birth.

As funny as it seems, that Christmas pageant was a great tool to help our Afghan friends better understand Christianity. Radio, Bibles and Christian literature, tapes and records are other media forms God has used to support person-to-person evangelism in Afghanistan.

When the first teachers arrived in Afghanistan in the late 1940s, Christian programs were broadcast in English over Radio Ceylon. It was possible to hear Billy Graham's "Hour of Decision," Charles Fuller's "Old-Fashioned Revival Hour," and the "Lutheran Hour." However, the Ceylon government changed, and Christian programs were taken off the air in the early 1950s.

For many years it was difficult to hear Christian broadcasts in Afghanistan. Although there was no freedom to preach the gospel locally, we in the Christian community felt truth could come in from outside the country via the media. Much prayer was offered for this need, and many ideas were considered.

We were thrilled in 1963, when the first programs in Dari were broadcast from the Voice of the Gospel in Addis Ababa, Ethiopia. Seven years later programs began reaching Afghanistan from a broadcasting station on the Seychelles Islands in the Indian Ocean. Then, after twenty years of praying and waiting, Radio Sri Lanka (Ceylon) once again began to air Christian broadcasts on their commercial service, reaching into Afghanistan as well as the whole Indian subcontinent. Some conversions have resulted from these Christian broadcasts.

Bible distribution has also produced gratifying results. In 1948 I attended the Olympic Games in London, and was intrigued to see a contingent of Afghan athletes marching around the track, dressed in their karakul caps. I prayed that somehow God would enable them to be reached with the message of eternal life.

I felt led to go to the British and Foreign Bible Society office in London and ask if they could give all the Olympic athletes Scripture portions in their own languages. They enthusiastically agreed and had New Testament covers printed with the Olympic symbol in gold leaf.

In Kabul some years later, a student asked me about a verse in a Persian New Testament he held in his hand. I answered him and then looked at the cover: on it were the golden rings of the Olympic Games! Words cannot express the excitement I felt as I returned home that afternoon. The Word of God had been brought back into Afghanistan by those athletes.

The reason for my enthusiasm was because both the Afghan and United States governments did everything within their power to keep Bibles outside the country. The State Department was afraid that Bibles brought into the country by Americans would offend the sensitive Afghan government—something that was to be avoided if at all possible.

One incident was particularly touchy. In August, 1957, we needed English Bibles for our church, and placed an order for them in Pakistan. The order came addressed to the treasurer of the church, Warren Smith, in care of the American embassy since this was the only address we had at the time. But when embassy officials realized the content of this package, the American ambassador threatened to send Warren and his family home at their own expense for smuggling Bibles into the country!

Our church board immediately wrote a letter to the ambassador, explaining that the Bibles had been ordered for church use. The board took full responsibility for the consignment. The ambassador understandably was quite touchy, since he had been in charge of the American embassy in Ecuador a year earlier when Jim Elliot and four other missionaries were killed by the Auca Indians. He had wanted to avoid another potential dangerous situation.

He called me into his office and accused me of plotting to smuggle Bibles into Afghanistan. I, in turn, explained that what we did was perfectly in order. I also expressed our church's disappointment with the U.S. government's policy of interference in such matters.

Angrily, he finally permitted the release of the shipment.

Since Kabul Community Christian was an international church, we stocked Scriptures in a variety of languages to meet the needs of persons in the international community. Even Russians came and bought Bibles to take back home to the Soviet Union with them.

Many Scriptures in the local languages were eventually given out on a friend-to-friend basis. We found that people, for the most part, were appreciative, because the Koran says the Christian and Jewish holy books of the Pentateuch, Psalms, and New

Testament are from God. Often people would lift the Scripture portion we gave them up to their lips and kiss it.

The church also provided a natural outlet for Christian literature. Over the years, many good books, pamphlets, and Bibles were sold. Texts of Scripture were framed and given to families in the international community as presents at Christmas. Consequently, Bible portions were hung in many international homes in Afghanistan.

But there were times when the reaction against Scripture distribution in Afghanistan was violent. So was the fate of Carl Nielsen, a Swedish missionary serving in Pakistan. He had visited Kabul with his wife and three children in the summer of 1971. As he had done quite freely in Pakistan, Carl gave a Pushtu Gospel of Luke to a storekeeper after making a purchase in the bazaar.

Another man saw him do this and asked if he could have a copy as well, and Carl obliged. But a bystander witnessed the exchange and began to fanatically shout *"Kafir!"* (unbeliever). A crowd gathered. The police were summoned, and Carl and his family were placed under room arrest in their hotel.

After two days his wife and children were free to come and go; but he was kept under twenty-four hour guard for two and one-half months while an official charge was prepared against him.

The accusation acknowledged that the New Testament was the Word of God, but contended that the Koran was the latest and all-sufficient revelation of God. Therefore, the New Testament was not needed, nor allowed in Afghanistan.

The charge also quoted Luke 3: 22: "and a voice came out of heaven, 'Thou art my beloved Son, in Thee I am well pleased.' " The accusation stated that the Koran revealed Jesus as the Son of Mary, and Carl's book said that he was the Son of God. It concluded that the Koran was right and the Gospel wrong.

The Muslim judge who had been assigned to the case, died suddenly. Many of the Afghans involved interpreted his death as a bad omen and were frightened. To make matters more complicated, a United Press International correspondent was visiting Kabul and heard about Carl's predicament. He interviewed the family in their hotel room and filed a story, which included a family picture. The feature was published in newspapers all over the world.

By the time another judge was chosen and the case was tried, the Afghan lawyer defended him so well that all religious charges were dropped. The defense centered on the Koran passages which acknowledge that the New Testament or *(Injil)* is the Word of God. Carl was simply fined the equivalent of twenty-five dollars for distributing literature without the sanction of the Ministry of Culture and Information.

Cassette tape recorders were becoming more and more common throughout Afghanistan. Recognizing this trend, the Kabul Community Christian Church purchased the necessary equipment, and developed a tape ministry. Messages from leading Christian men and women around the world were recorded. These were made available in a lending library for anyone who wanted to borrow them. Many of the church services were recorded and sent to different parts of the country. Small fellowship groups of Christians in Kandahar, Lashkar Gah, Herat, Panjao, Nyak, Mazari-Sharif, and Jalalabad often gathered to use them in their worship.

Still, we had very little to offer Afghan nationals. And so in March of 1967 we commenced a recording project of major proportions. Nell Gibson, with Gospel Recordings of India, came to Afghanistan, and taped gospel messages in the two main languages, Dari and Pushtu. That left fifty languages to go, which is precisely what we prayed for. We were determined to record and distribute gospel messages in all of Afghanistan's fifty-two tongues. Later that year I was able to arrange for Ann Sherwood and Marlene Muhr, also with Gospel Recordings, to come to Afghanistan in late 1969 and help us record Christian messages in more languages.

But the difficulties seemed insurmountable. One of the young Uzbeki men we were using in our recording session refused to repeat the fact that Jesus Christ had died on the cross, since he said he did not believe it. We had to let him go. Another Uzbeki speaker was sought who would be willing to tell the gospel. God gave us just the right man, who happened to have a far better voice and delivery than the first.

Once we traveled to the border of Nuristan where we were met by two men from inaccessible tribes. After everyone else in the home where we were staying had gone to bed, we spent the entire night recording gospel messages in their two languages.

At dawn we paid them for their expenses and help, and sent them off on their three-day journey by foot back to their valleys. It soon became evident, however, that traveling to such inaccessible areas would be difficult and dangerous if what we were doing was discovered by the Muslim government. So Afghan Christians helped us to locate soldiers in Kabul, who had been drafted into the army from all parts of the country and represented all of the language groups. We also used students who came to the capital from outlying areas.

End result? All fifty-two languages were recorded during the four months Miss Sherwood and Miss Muhr were in the country and three months later, all of these messages had been pressed onto records.

For most people listening to these recordings, it was the first time they had heard the story of Christ. Many people wondered why no one had told them this before.

I now realize why God had led us in making those gospel recordings. We weren't aware of it at the time, but our work in Afghanistan was rapidly approaching its end. Pressure was building on Afghanistan's leaders to destroy the Kabul Community Christian Church and banish all foreign Christians from the country.

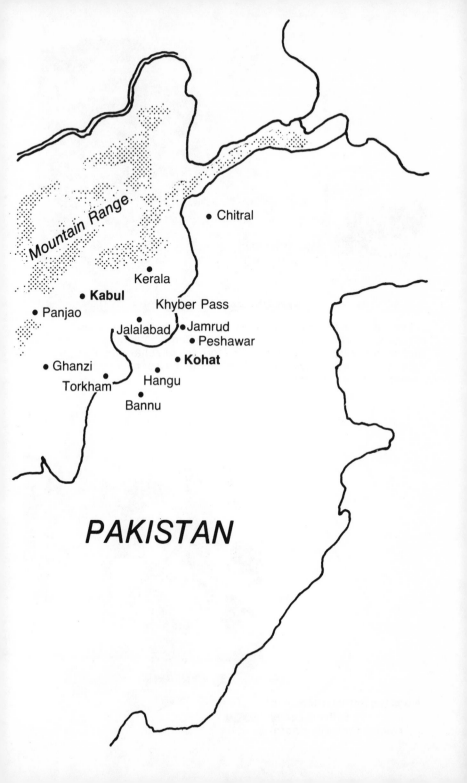

Even today, camel caravans are the only way to bring supplies to remote Afghan areas. This river is in the Bamian Valley in Afghanistan's central highlands. The fortress of Zohak (upper right) was destroyed by Genghis Khan in the thirteenth century. *(James Cudney—photo)*

Nomadic Pathan tribesman
with his camel
(James Cudney—photo)

Afghanistan's strategic importance has been recognized by both the United States and the Soviet Union. Here, Russian Premier Nikita Khrushchev visits Kabul in 1955. Afghan Prime Minister Mohammed Daoud looks on as Khrushchev announces à 100 million dollar loan to Afghanistan at 2 percent interest. *(James Cudney—photo)*

Pathan tribesmen, many of whom are fighting with the *mujahiddin* ("freedom fighters") are recognized as some of the best marksmen in the world. *(James Cudney—photo)*

Over 1 million Afghan refugees are living in crowded and dirty conditions in Pakistan, clinging to the hope that they will one day be able to return to their homeland.

Flora Davidson—A great woman of faith who served almost forty years on Afghanistan's borders.

Literacy expert, Dr. Frank Laubach, works late into the night on Afghan reading primers (March, 1951). Here, he sits on a table to make the most of the lone lightbulb in his dim hotel room.

Doctor Kinston Keh, Chinese agricultural expert, holds a Long Island Duckling. This breed of fowl was first introduced to Afghanistan in the late 1950s.

Betty Wilson during construction of the Kabul Community Christian Church.

Dedication service—Kabul Community Christian Church (May 17, 1970).

Cornerstone—Kabul Community Christian Church

Brother Andrew, "God's Smuggler," prays at the Kabul
Community Christian Church. Christy Wilson (right).

View of the Kabul Community Christian Church shortly after its front wall was destroyed by Afghan soldiers (February, 1973).

Russian-built bulldozers put the finishing touches on the Kabul Community Christian Church demolition (July, 1973).

8
The Stone the Builders Rejected

"In the ditch where water has flowed, it will flow again." [*ba joee aw (awb) rafta bawshad bawz khawt awmad.*]

Afghan proverb

"The Afghanistan government has informed me that they are preparing a list of around ten people who will be ordered to leave the country. I don't know the names, but I'm sure you and your wife will be at the top."

This was the message United States Ambassador Robert Neumann relayed to me in the middle of March, 1973. Surprisingly though, our names were not on the list. It was comprised mainly of the other staff members at the Institute for the Blind. More Afghans had come to Christ through this ministry than any other and the Afghans were determined to rid themselves of the "corrupting influence."

A few days later, Ambassador Neumann asked the Afghanistan minister of interior why Betty and I had not been included. He admitted that we would have headed the list had I not once taught English to King Zahir Shah's son, the crown prince. Apparently Prime Minister Shafiq feared that his decision would be overruled.

We had been given a temporary reprieve, but Neumann warned us that Shafiq wanted us out. He let me know in no uncertain terms that the Americans could take no responsibility for our safety. Ambassador Neumann left the choice of whether or not to leave up to me, and I must admit his word of warning came back to haunt me during the next few days. Betty and I had a real sense of uneasiness about staying in Afghanistan.

During morning devotions on March 19, 1973, we read Deuteronomy 1:6, "The Lord our God spoke to us at Horeb, saying, 'You have stayed long enough at this mountain.' " We also read the passage in Luke 9:5 when Jesus told his disciples that there would be occasions where it would be best to shake the dust from your feet when people do not receive you as Christ's messengers. It was evident to us that God's time had come for us to leave the country, and with the blessing of the Kabul Community Christian Church leaders, my wife and I walked on Afghan soil for the last time on March 24, 1973.

The timing of our departure proved to be a godsend for two reasons. First, we arrived in California just in time to spend my father's last three days on earth at his bedside. Second, we later learned that some Muslim zealots had been involved in an assassination plot against our lives. One way or another, our days in Afghanistan had been numbered.

Though leaving Afghanistan was a great disappointment, the biggest disappointment of my life happened three months later. I was attending a Midwest missions conference and was freshening up before the evening meal in my motel room. I crossed the room to answer the ringing telephone. Never will I forget those next few agonizing minutes. . . .

"Christy, I'm afraid I have some very bad news." It was Ray Knighton, president of MAP International. "I just got a call from the State Department in Washington. Word from Kabul is not very good. Apparently, the Afghan government has authorized the destruction of the church building. . . . Bulldozers and a demolition crew entered the compound today and are making every effort to reduce the building to a pile of rubble. . . ."

I slowly hung up the motel phone in a state of shock, not believing what I had just heard. The State Department had informed Ray that the fight to save the Kabul Community Christian Church had been lost.

When Betty and I had returned to the United States the previous March we had hoped our involuntary furlough in

America would be short, and it would soon be safe to return to our duties with the Kabul Community Christian Church. Now those prospects looked bleak.

Overwhelming grief swept over me and a tidal wave of emotion poured from my body. I wept uncontrollably before the Lord, facedown on the motel carpet. All I could think about was the time, effort, and sacrifice that had gone into the erection of that building. Literally thousands of people had unselfishly contributed their prayers, financial resources, and physical labor, so Christians in Afghanistan's capital city could have a place to worship the Lord together. Now, three short years after its dedication, the building was being destroyed.

Why? It just didn't make sense.

It was one of the hardest things I ever did, but I thanked the Lord through my tears, knowing that somehow, he was still in charge and would be glorified through it all. Slowly, a calming peace enveloped me. Then, Christ's words in John 12:24, came to mind, "Truly, truly, I say to you, unless a grain of wheat falls into the earth and dies, it remains by itself alone; but if it dies, it bears much fruit."

". . . but if it dies, it bears much fruit." God had spoken gently. I knew that even though this building was destroyed, our efforts had not been in vain. I knew the Lord could raise up many Afghan churches and followers of Christ in the future. But I couldn't help letting my mind drift back to the past; back to my early ministry amongst the Kabul international community in the mid-1950s; back when the thought of erecting a Christian church building on Afghan soil was only a dream. . . .

The need for a church facility had immediately become evident. Few living rooms were large enough to accommodate the numbers of foreigners from abroad who wanted to worship together. To make matters worse, a succession of landlords had charged exorbitant rents to the non-Muslims using their property. Many uncommitted Christians declined invitations to attend home meetings, arguing that since Afghanistan's government had not given permission for a church building, they might be viewed suspiciously for attending the house services.

Beginning in 1956, Kabul Christians had prayed regularly for permission to put up a place of worship. A letter to the Afghan Cabinet was drafted in 1957 requesting approval to secure property and erect a building. We knew that no non-Afghan is allowed to own property in Afghanistan, so the request was for a ninety-nine year lease—the same arrangement secured by foreign embassies.

Our request had been denied.

But that didn't stop us from trying again. Two years later we were helped by the clout of the world's most influencial person. Dwight Eisenhower was to become the first United States president to visit Afghanistan. Hoping to capitalize on a golden opportunity, I wrote his pastor in Washington, Dr. Edward R. Elson, and urged him to speak to the president about our request to build a church. The Islamic mosque in Washington had just been dedicated, and President Eisenhower had been present for the occasion.

It seemed only fair that if Muslim diplomats and foreign service personnel now had a place to worship in the American capital, Christian diplomats and other foreigners should be allowed a place of worship in Kabul.

Doctor Elson, who later would spend almost two decades as chaplain of the United States Senate, replied with good news. The White House had agreed.

President Eisenhower was only in Afghanistan for four and one-half hours, and political matters took up most of his time. Still, he made good on his word and mentioned the church matter to the king. American Ambassador Henry Byroade then followed up on the president's request with the Afghan government.

In 1960, the long-awaited OK finally arrived. But there was a catch. Permission was given to build if the structure were put on some embassy property, a clause similar to an agreement that had allowed a Roman Catholic chapel to be built at the Italian embassy in 1955, five years earlier.

Needless to say, our congregation was disappointed. We felt that since we had an international membership, it would be preferable to locate our building on neutral soil. The mosque in Washington had been built on private land, and it was felt that building at one particular embassy would limit our ministry to only a segment of the foreign community.

The Afghan government in turn had feared that granting permission for a Protestant church on private property could cause real problems. Muslim reactionaries had been rioting because women had been allowed to remove their tentlike veil (*burka*) in public. The Afghan officials wanted some time to let things cool off. They asked that the request be renewed later, and indicated that permission would be given.

Six long years passed as one excuse after another was given for the delay. Finally on June 16, 1966, verbal permission was given by the prime minister's office to build the church and secure property on a *girau* or long-term mortgage basis. The Afghan Cabinet secretary told the Municipality of Kabul to approve the plans.

Elated by the news, our congregation voted unanimously to secure property and build and it wasn't long before we were full speed ahead with the project. A planning committee commenced a thorough study of the building's size and whether it should be of arabesque, Western, or modern architecture.

Thomas Haughey, who was president of the New Zealand Association of Architects, visited Afghanistan in March of 1968, and was requested to draw up plans on the basis of the planning committee's recommendations. He submitted his proposed style, a motif that accented Kabul's surrounding mountains, and the congregation, on May 29, 1968, voted unanimously that he should go ahead with his blueprints. Later, an Afghan architect, who was a graduate of the University of Pennsylvania and was in charge of all Kabul construction, looked over the plans and endorsed them. He said that this was just the kind of church he would have liked to have designed for Kabul.

But the church was not without its opponents. Great controversy surrounded the building of the structure, especially in the international community. Certain people, most of whom were not church members or contributors, strongly objected to the expenditures, as well as the architectural style.

Some said that the money should have been given to the poor. Others felt that the cost was far too much, and that a church of four adobe walls and a galvanized roof would be adequate. (We felt that in order to attract non-Christians in the diplomatic and United Nations communities, an architecturally attractive building would be helpful.) Still others held the opinion that it should be in the shape of a domed mosque. Some thought it would be too large for our needs, and others said it should not be started until all the money was raised, lest we not be able to finish.

Despite the criticism, the church membership was strongly committed to the building program. In April, 1969, the congregation voted to go ahead with the construction, with only one dissenting vote. We prayed in faith, believing for the needed funds, and God wonderfully answered those prayers.

People all over the world contributed. A little seventeen-member congregation in Japan sent a gift of ten dollars. Christian students in Korea collected the equivalent of fifteen dollars. One Christian woman, from a country behind the Iron Curtain, slipped into the church office and left a contribution.

"I'm sorry I can't come to your services," she said to me. "I'm being watched very closely." But she was so glad permission had been given to build a church, she wanted to have a part in it!

An elderly Christian woman once arrived at the Kabul Airport unexpectedly and phoned me, asking to see the plans for the new church. She said that she was traveling around the world looking for worthy causes to donate her money to, before she died. At that time we were twenty thousand dollars short of our goal. She graciously gave the full amount!

Our construction engineer, John Reoch of Toronto, Canada, was a dedicated Christian layman. He arrived just before ground for the new building was broken in July, 1969. The Bishop of Lahore, Pakistan, the Right Reverend Iniyat Massih, and Ellen Rasmussen (representing the many who had prayed, witnessed, and suffered on the frontiers—see chapter 10) turned over the first sod. The building went up in less than a year, and on Pentecost Sunday, 1970, hundreds gathered for dedication ceremonies. Doctor Ted Engstrom, executive vice-president of World Vision International, and Mrs. Jean Darnell from the Festival of Light in England gave the main messages.

A Christian ophthalmologist from Scotland, Dr. Murray McGavin, sang from Psalm 84: "How amiable are thy tabernacles, O Lord of hosts. . . . Yea the sparrow hath found a house . . . even thine altars." While he sang, sparrows happily flew around to their nests inside the new building, since the doors and windows had not yet been installed.

But the euphoria surrounding the dedication was short-lived. Eight days after the ceremonies, I received a court order from the municipality of Kabul. All construction was to stop immediately!

The Afghan government had been extremely nervous about any visible non-Muslim influence. At that time, thousands of *mullahs* had been demonstrating in Kabul regarding another matter. Russia was celebrating the one hundredth anniversary of Lenin's birth, and in order to demonstrate friendship with her neighbor to the north, Afghanistan had allowed articles describing the event to appear in the government newspapers.

Unfortunately, one editor had gotten over-enthusiastic. At the end of his article, he had written a prayer for Lenin's soul, asking God to forgive him! This immediately provoked a violent reaction among the *mullahs* who converged by the thousands on Kabul from all parts of the country.

"No one had the right to pray for Lenin's soul," they said, "when he had been responsible for leading so many Muslims astray into atheism."

The *mullahs* demanded the execution of the newspaper editor and the Minister of Culture and Information. The demonstrators then had criticized the king as an unbeliever and turned against the government. Demonstration leaders were arrested and the others were sent home. But the government still had deemed it unwise to allow the church construction to continue.

Though disappointed, the congregation remained hopeful and viewed this final delay as a chance once again to grow in faith. The cold central Asian winds made it a bit drafty at times, but we were able to use the unfinished building for services, baptisms, and weddings. Many people from throughout the world wrote to offer encouragement, including Corrie ten Boom of the Netherlands. Finally, almost a year later, in April, 1971, after much fasting and prayer, the government gave us the green light to put the finishing touches on the building.

The completed church served our needs well, and attendance increased to an average of over two hundred for morning services. Many new members joined and others had the rare privilege of hearing the Word of God in a Muslim country.

Several special activities highlighted the church calendar. For example, in the spring of 1972, while we were on furlough in the States, there was a wonderful revival in Kabul under the ministry of Dr. Raymond Ortlund, who was then pastor of Lake Avenue Congregational Church in Pasadena, California. Many people in attendance confessed their sins openly and made things right with one another.

But those were tense times in Afghanistan and the months did not pass by without trouble. Government leadership was now split into two factions. There were the hard-core Muslims who were determined to keep the country pure of non-Islamic influence. The second faction saw the value of close relations with Westerners. Sometimes the government would say one thing, and then do another and vice versa. We were never quite sure what would happen.

On Sunday morning September 13, 1972, forty soldiers began attacking the wall that separated the church property from the street. American Ambassador John Neumann took the matter directly to the king, so we thought there would be no further trouble.

Then on February 25, 1973, the church wall was again attacked without warning, and completely destroyed. This time, the American ambassador was in Germany for a physical checkup.

We called an emergency meeting and prayed for God's guidance to help us handle the situation. One of our church leaders, an influential Christian businessman went to the Mayor of Kabul. He left the word of warning that if his government touched the "house of God," they would be judged. Diplomats from many nations approached the authorities and the Afghan government agreed to a ten-day, and then one-month, grace period so that the matter could be discussed. Three members of the church were appointed to negotiate with the government, but several efforts to reason with the authorities were of no avail.

Dost Mohammed Fazl, acting mayor of Kabul, sent the church board an expropriation notice shortly after Betty and I left the country:

From the morning of Wednesday, 23rd Jawza, 1352 (June 13, 1973) the roof of the church will be destroyed by the Kabul Municipality. The building, in accordance with the decision of the higher authorities, will be used by the Kabul

Municipality for other purposes. From the above-mentioned day no one has any right to enter the building or premises of the church. Whoever enters will be punished as a violator of Afghan laws. The final day above has been announced to you.

The church trustees each stared at the expropriation notice with disbelief. Sensing that the church might never be able to use the facility again, they responded to the notice and placed a claim for compensation:

Is this holy place of prayer, which was consecrated in the sight of God, going to be destroyed? Will devout Muslims really feel that this is the way to treat the people of the Book? As Christians, we shall not resist: first, because our Holy Book commands us to pray for, honor, and obey those who have the power to rule over us. But, second because, although this beautiful building is of great value in terms of the investment of money and effort put into it, there are other values which we prize more highly—such as peace and goodwill among men, freedom of conscience, respect for the rights and beliefs of others. . . . How can we, in all conscience give this building for its demolition, since it is dedicated to the glory of God? We cannot of ourselves accept responsibility for such a thing, for we are only trustees of that for which others have given and labored. The action taken will be the responsibility of the Royal Afghan Government.

Unfortunately, the document had no effect on the Afghan officials. They were determined that no Christian would ever step inside the building again, and on June 14, 1973, bulldozers began their assault on the abandoned building.

It's difficult to find anything humorous in this sad story; especially since that building had become an integral part of my life for almost two decades. But I have since gotten a small chuckle from this incident.

Afghan officials had always seemed to be suspicious of the church building. Apparently, the Russian embassy had complained to the Afghan government about alleged "secret listening devices" hidden in the church. (The Russian embassy had been only two hundred meters up the street.) Our simultaneous translation system had given rise to the rumor that we were eavesdropping on Russian conversations. This system, which had the capability of interpreting church messages in different languages, was a maze of lights, dials, and wires and it was easy to see how the rumor had gotten started.

The Afghan secret service had also picked up a report that there was an "underground church" in Afghanistan. They had felt certain that there must be some subterranean secret meeting place under our building. Afghan workers carefully dug below the demolished building's foundation in a futile search for the "hidden church."

My time in Afghanistan had ended, and someday I hope to return to the people and country I have grown to love. But my story is only a small part of God's plan for Afghanistan. Many had gone before me, and many have followed, endeavoring to sow the seed of God's Truth in this land of the forbidden harvest.

9
"Mullah Jousuf"

"The seeker is the finder." [*joyinda yawbinda as(t).*]

Afghan proverb

One thousand years ago, there were more people in Asia who called themselves Christians than there were in all of Europe and the rest of the world put together. Crosses, still woven in Afghan carpets, witness to the past Christian era, and old coins bare the legend, "In the name of the Father, Son, and Holy Ghost, one God."[1]

Unfortunately, little recognition has been given to the Eastern Christian churches because most of European Christendom wrote them off as heretics. Western students of church history from the fifth to fifteenth centuries usually ignored the Eastern church.

This feeling dated back to a fifth-century controversy between Cyril, Bishop of Alexandria, and Nestorius, Bishop of Constantinople. Cyril's followers held that Christ's two natures, divine and human, became one (monophysitism). Nestorius agreed that Christ did have two natures, but they were "united," not unified (dyophysitism).

And so the Eastern and Western church split over this

theological squabble. Had that division not occurred, Asia might be the predominantly Christian part of the world today, rather than the West.

Several factors contributed to the decline of the Asian church as history moved into the second millennium after Christ. Nestorian missionaries kept the Word of God in Syriac, rather than translating it into the language of the people. The Bible eventually became a "closed book," while there was a growing decadence among clergy who, not being regenerated through an understanding of the gospel, became corrupt—usurers, drunkards, and polygamists.

The scourge of conquerors like Genghis Khan also contributed to the demise of Christianity as a vital force in Asia. Genghis Khan ruthlessly slaughtered one million people in Afghanistan's Herat Valley, a strong center of Christianity, in the thirteenth century. Even today one of Herat's suburbs is called *Injil,* which means gospel.

Slowly but surely, the ever-powerful influence of Islam began to make its way eastward. In 1747, when Pathan tribal leader Ahmad Shah declared much of what is now Afghanistan a nation, most tribes inhabiting the country were solid adherents to the ways of Islam. Any influence of Christianity had become all but extinct in the mountains, plains, and valleys of Afghanistan.

The nineteenth century brought with it the dawn of the modern missionary movement. Many servants of God were determined to loosen Islam's grip on the people of central Asia. Two of these most zealous pioneer missionaries were Henry Martyn and William Carey. Though neither had ever set foot in Afghanistan, they were largely responsible for Scripture translations into the two principal languages of the country, Dari and Pushtu.

Henry Martyn arrived in India in 1806 to serve as chaplain for the East India Company. There he commenced his first major translation project—the New Testament into Hindustani.

Five years later, he set sail for Shiraz in southern Iran. Headquartered there, he worked on a revision of the Persian New Testament from June, 1811, to February, 1812. On completion, he presented a beautifully handwritten copy to Iranian King Fath Ali Shah, who wrote, "If it pleases the most merciful God, we shall select servants to read to us the book from beginning to end.''

Martyn was so committed to the cause of the gospel, he reportedly once said, ''I have lived more like a clod of dirt than like a son of God. Now let me burn out for Christ.''

And that's just what happened. He died in October, 1812, a victim of disease and exhaustion. It was written of him, ''Rarely has the world seen such a combination of superior scholarship and dedicated devotion to Christ.''

William Carey also had a great burden for the people of Afghanistan. Sometimes referred to as ''the father of the modern missionary movement,'' Carey spent most of his life telling the gospel message to the people of India. He took a real interest in the Pathan people of northern India, and translated the entire Bible into Pushtu. It was published in a five-volume edition in 1818.

The first modern missionary to actually preach in Afghanistan was Dr. Joseph Wolff. Born in 1795, the son of a Jewish rabbi in Bavaria, he accepted Christ as his Savior, and enrolled at England's Cambridge University. With a courage and commitment equaled by few men he set out for Asia in 1821. His itinerary included Turkey, Iran (Persia), and in subsequent journeys he also visited Bokhara (now a part of southern Russia), Afghanistan, and India.

Wherever he went, he proclaimed himself a ''Christian dervish'' or ''mullah Jousuf'' (the Islamic term for a religious teacher named Joseph). Boldly he witnessed to Muslims and Jews. When heading into potentially dangerous areas, Joseph secured letters of introduction to local leaders from their friends, whom he'd met earlier along the way.

Joseph Wolff made a second missionary journey from 1831 to 1834 and preached his way through Afghanistan. Often Muslim leaders would ask him his profession. Proudly, he'd lift up a copy of the Scriptures and would answer in Persian, ''This is my profession, proclaiming the Bible and the gospel among the Jews and to converse with all nations about God.''[2]

Once in a central Afghanistan village, his servant was asked, ''Is Dr. Wolff a Muslim?''

The servant replied, ''Yes.''

But Dr. Wolff, overheard the conversation and spoke up,

"No, I am a believer in Jesus Christ."

That did not go over very well with the town chief of Duab. As a test, the chief demanded that Dr. Wolff repeat the Muslim creed, which of course, he refused to do.

This aroused the ire of the local Muslim *mullahs* who sentenced him to burn at the stake. However, God had much more planned for Joseph Wolff's life, and the *mullahs* finally agreed to free him if he would give them all he had. So Dr. Wolff left his modest wardrobe behind, and went on his way in rags.

He eventually reached a village near Kabul on Monday, April 30, 1832. But everything seemed hopeless. He still had no clothing or money and his muleteer imprisoned him in a mud house, until Wolff paid the travel fee. In spite of his discouraging circumstances he wrote in his diary, "I prayed to Jesus Christ, my Savior, who never left a prayer of mine unheard, to assist me in my present trouble."

Within hours his servant, whom he'd sent to Kabul, returned with a horse, new clothes, and a letter from Lieutenant Alexander Burns, the British political agent who providentially had arrived in Kabul not long before. Lieutenant Burns assured Dr. Wolff that he would receive every assistance and invited him to stay with the British party during his Kabul visit. Through Burns, Dr. Wolff received an audience with the king of Afghanistan, Amir Dost Mohammed.

Doctor Joseph Wolff had traveled over Afghanistan's rugged mountains and scorching deserts voluntarily. Others made their way over Afghanistan's mountain passes because they had to.

Britain governed most of southcentral Asia during the 1800s. Viewing Afghanistan as a strategic buffer between Czarist Russia and India (Britain's most valuable piece of real estate), English troops invaded and occupied several Afghan cities for a number of years in the 1830s and 1840s. Consequently, some of the finest witnesses in Afghanistan were the Christian officers and soldiers of the British Army.

Christian servicemen stationed in Herat met regularly for prayer, and distributed copies of William Carey's Pushtu New Testament to their Afghan friends. The Kabul regiment also had its share of believers. One soldier, a Captain Reban, ordered a shipment of Bibles. When the Bibles arrived in Kabul, they were confiscated by the British authorities. They were fearful of anything which might inflame the local Muslims. The Bibles were sent back on the next caravan out of the country which was promptly attacked and looted in a narrow pass. Doctor Harry Holland wrote, "The Word of God was scattered, not for the last time, up and down that stony ground."[3]

Another British officer, Captain Arthur Conolly, wrote, "God seems now to be breaking up all barriers of the long-closed East for the introduction of Christian knowledge and peace."[4]

In 1840, the commander of the Herat regiment, Colonel Stoddart was captured and imprisoned by the king of Bokhara. The colonel's crime had simply been refusing to become a Muslim. Captain Conolly made the trip north to try to effect Colonel Stoddart's release. He, too, was imprisoned and thrown into a dungeon along with the colonel. Conditions were pathetic as vermin and sheep ticks bored into their flesh, but nothing could stop their enthusiasm for the Lord. Conolly managed to sneak an Anglican Prayer Book into the prison with him. He wrote the following message in the margin:

"Thank God that this prayer book was left to me. Stoddart and I have found it a great comfort. We did not know fully before this affliction what was in the Psalms or how beautiful were the prayers of the church. Nothing but the spirit of Christianity can heal the wickedness and misery in these countries."[5]

Neither man lived to see their freedom as shortly thereafter, each man lost his head to the blade of a sword.

Three years passed without word from the Christian officers, so Dr. Wolff made the trip north to Bokhara. He was determined to find out what had happened to the two men. When he learned of their death he donned his clerical robes, his scarlet doctor's hood, and a shovel hat. He then entered the city of Bokhara carrying a large open Bible in front of him. Joseph Wolff had a way of attracting attention, and once again he was at his best. People questioning the stranger about his unusual outfit heard this reply: "The black robes are in mourning for the death of two friends. The red hood symbolizes that I am not afraid to shed my blood for Christ either."

Joseph Wolff's life was spared and he returned to England to tell the story of the two brave British officers. But many others did not live to return to England. The mid-1840s saw British troops locked in a bitter war with Afghan tribal warriors. Thousands died and the British soldiers were forced to withdraw from the country. Afghanistan, temporarily free of foreign influence, adopted a policy of isolationism. This fit in well with the British policy of keeping the country a no-man's-land between India and Russia. Almost all outsiders, including Christian missionaries, were barred from the country for nearly a century.

10
Kohat's Great Lover

"The first day you meet you are friends, the next day you meet you are brothers." [*yag roz deedee dost digar roz deedee birawdar.*]
Afghan proverb

Christian activity inside Afghanistan was held almost entirely in check from the 1840s until the mid-1940s. But that didn't stop dedicated missionaries from influencing Afghan citizens who traveled to nearby cities, towns, and villages across the border.

Peshawar, Pakistan (India before 1947), because of its strategic location at the eastern entrance of the Khyber Pass, became a Christian center for reaching Afghans. Many passed through Peshawar on their pilgrimage to Mecca. Others traded in the Peshawar bazaar or were there on Afghanistan government business. Peshawar was one in a chain of strategically located mission stations, extending all the way from Chinese Turkestan near Afghanistan's northeast border, to Mashad, Iran, near the northwest border.

Kohat, near Peshawar, was a notable outpost. A Christian witness was established there as a result of the prayer and dedication of English servicemen. In 1923, a group of inquirers came to a Christian officer stationed there with the British Army. He instructed them in the faith, and some of them were then baptized. They formed the nucleus of the Hindustani church in Kohat, headed later by the enthusiastic Miss Flora Davidson.

Flora came from Aberdeen, Scotland, where her mother had become a Christian during the Dwight L. Moody and Ira Sankey evangelistic campaign in the 1880s. Her father was a laird who, after a spectacular conversion, went around the countryside with a large tent preaching the gospel.

In 1909, Flora Davidson went to Peshawar to visit her brother, a soldier who was serving on the frontier with a high-land regiment. While she was there, she became burdened to return and work for Christ among the people of that area. When Flora returned to England, she announced her plans to return. However, her family and friends feared for her health, and insisted that she first spend a two-year trial period in Bangalore in southern India.

Flora set sail for India again in 1912, and spent her time in Bangalore engrossed in language study. She then packed her bags and proceeded to Mardan where she worked with Dr. Marie Holst in the Danish Mission Hospital. Following a short stay in Mardan, Flora moved on to her original destination—Peshawar. She served as an evangelist with the Church of England Zenana Mission Hospital in Peshawar where she rented a house in the old city so she could be more accessible to the women. She called her home "The Cave of Adullum," named after the place where King David often found refuge as a young man.[1]

"I want everyone in need to feel this is a place for them," she had said.

During the third Anglo-Afghan War in 1919, which resulted in Afghanistan's complete independence from Britain, Flora Davidson nursed the wounded and sick in the Peshawar Military Hospital. Then in 1925, she moved to Kohat where she worked as a midwife, visited in homes and villages, and shared the gospel wherever possible. She was even able to get into tribal areas usually off limits to missionaries.

She built a small home in the city proper, which she opened to visitors. A Danish nurse, Miss Maria Rasmussen, lived and worked with her there.

Afghanistan, however, remained tightly closed to any followers of Christ. Flora Davidson's entrance applications were denied time after time. But she continued to witness in the Kohat district. In 1938 she wrote: "These last two winters I have concentrated on the villages. We soon shall have preached the gospel in every good-sized village in the district." In the outlying hamlets, she met with the women, helped them with their physical ailments, and shared the good news of Jesus Christ.

Flora describes her meeting with the women of Kilazek, a small village:

> After the first shyness had worn off, they showered questions upon their visitor. They fingered the odd foreign clothes and wanted to know the price of each material. They plucked at a bit of brown stocking, asking if it were skin!
>
> "Are you really a woman?" questioned one. "Everyone tells us you are a man in disguise!"
>
> "How many children have you?" asked another.
>
> The visitor needed only to put her thumb to her chin, and then wave her hand in the air to indicate that she was not married or "owned no bearded one"!
>
> "How is it that God has blessed you that you have no husband?"[2]

But in 1939, Miss Davidson was banned from Kohat. Her offense? Twelve persons had confessed Christ in that city! She was viewed as a corrupting influence on the community.

God then enabled her to open medical work in Hangu, twenty-six miles to the west, toward Parichinar on the Afghan border. Again, she was ordered out by the deputy commissioner of Kohat district, who labeled it a "dangerous area."

So famous did Flora become, that at one time a bounty of 5,000 rupees was put on her head. The British authorities were concerned for her safety and mandated that she have four armed guards around her day and night. Reluctantly she submitted to the order. However, without telling anyone else, she refused to let them have any ammunition.

The years went on and Flora continued to carry her joyous witness to villages all along the frontier. In 1942 she wrote:

> "It was a glorious evening. We were close under the rugged Mohmand hills. The welcome and loving greetings of the women were still sounding warm in my ears. The men in

the family were walking back with me—a Pathan politeness.

"As we came along the Kabul riverbank, one of the men sighted some duck, and went off to stalk them. We all sat down to wait, and they asked me to tell them what I had been telling the women in the house."[3]

Those who remained forgot about the hunt. Only the ripple of the Kabul River broke the hush that fell on them as again the old, old story of the Savior was listened to in that faraway corner of the northwest frontier province.

"Ah! but it's wonderful," one man remarked. "There is no other story like that!"[4]

Ten years later, Flora was allowed to go back to the Kohat district. A friend described her welcome:

Men who had threatened, scowled, muttered, and closed the door a decade before, leapt from their shops to grasp her hand in welcome. Women in thick veils threw their arms around her neck crying, "Don't you remember me?"

Kohat's great lover had returned. Each day closed with this loving one on her knees with tears and prayers interceding for the ones who had gone astray and for the ones who had not come to know that they might have life.[5]

Margaret Ballantyne of the United Presbyterian Mission tells about taking a trip with Flora by bus from Kohat to Peshawar. She recounts:

There was another passenger in the front seat with her, but he had to give up his place to a tribal chief replete with cartridge belt and haughty mien. At once Miss Davidson began talking with him about salvation.

His expression as he gazed aghast at her boldness was a mixture of outrage, amazement, and admiration. Before she had finished speaking, his journey came to an end, and the driver stopped the bus to let him out.

But Miss Davidson said, "Wait, I am not through yet."

With the whole bus full of people listening awestruck, she kept that chief standing till she had completed telling him of the only Savior of his soul. Then thrusting a Gospel portion in his hand with the stern injunction to read it, she bade him good-bye and signaled the driver to proceed. The last glimpse of the proud old chief showed him staring at her with "Woman, you have courage!" gleaming from his eyes.[6]

Courage indeed. Flora feared no one. Her brother-in-law, General Thompson, had been knighted for his outstanding service to Britain. When offered the position of British Governor of the Northwest, he declined. He said he had no doubt that he could control the wild tribesmen in the area. It was his sister-in-law he was worried about.

In the summer of 1929, Flora Davidson and Maria Rasmussen traveled all along the borders of Afghanistan to meet personally those who were encircling that country with prayer. They visited Christians along the frontier and in cities such as Quetta, Baluchistan. They took a train to Duzdab (Zahidan) in southeastern Iran. There they met with friends at the Bible Churchmen's Missionary Society who were praying constantly for the opening of Afghanistan.

Prayer was Flora Davidson's secret weapon for the more than forty years she spent in Asia. In Kohat she had an "upper room," with a window like Daniel's, which looked out on the mountains of Afghanistan. In front of the window there was a little wooden bench, where she spent hour after hour on her knees, calling upon God to open the closed land to his gospel.

Flora and others were so burdened for the opening of Afghanistan that they organized a quarterly publication to encourage intercessary prayer. It was called the *Afghan Prayer Circle*. The first issue came out in the summer of 1924.

Special circles for prayer were organized in India, Denmark, England, Scotland, and the United States. Those who were enlisted were called "rope holders" and each was given a number.

Flora Davidson invited Christian servicemen in the British Army to a weekly prayer meeting in Kohat, which one sergeant called "a little powerhouse." Flora observed, "The opening of Afghanistan to the gospel is not yet attained, but we know our prayers are on the altar, and one day they will be answered in God's wonderful way."[7]

One of Flora's friends, Dr. Stapleton, who served in the hospital in Bannu as well as in Kashmir, observed:

Afghanistan is locked, barred, and bolted—against what? Against the gospel of Jesus Christ; the one thing that could make this great, restless, and fascinating land, a beautiful, peaceful, and powerful land. Prayer forced open the iron gate for Saint Peter to escape; and prayer can and will force open the iron gates that check the entrance of the gospel into Afghanistan.[8]

In January, 1938, the last issue of the *Afghan Prayer Circle* rolled off the presses. It was followed in April by a prayer quarterly, *Missions on the Borders of Afghanistan,* edited by Miss Margaret Haines. Margaret Haines had worked with Flora Davidson in Kohat from 1932-35, but had to return to the United States because of ill health. The quarterly was issued for twenty-one more years.

In 1959, Margaret changed the format to a monthly prayer letter, sent to over five hundred praying people. Since January, 1973, the prayer letter has been sent out by Bruce and Marilyn Clark, who taught in Afghanistan during the 1950s.

Flora Davidson herself was finally able to go to Afghanistan during the summer of 1949—the fulfillment of her lifelong dream. Her passport read "spinster," since she was a financially independent, unmarried woman. Officials apparently misunderstood the word *spinster* and thought it meant some kind of textile spinner or weaver, so they gave her a visa.

The four months she spent in Afghanistan were very pleasant. She loved poking about in the old bazaar, strolling around the public gardens, and making friends with the women and children. She lived in a funny house that former King Amir Amanullah had built for his little sister, and the upstairs sitting room had a beautiful view. People seemed to like coming there.

But it was really on the way to Mazar-i-Shariff that she saw the Afghanistan of her imaginings. The landscape was beautiful. The road ran next to the riverbank through magnificent gorges, and towering hills and scores of snow-covered peaks sparkled in the distance.

After slowly winding their way for miles, the group that she was traveling with came through a cleft in the rocks onto an enormous plain, stretching away into the distance further than the eye could see.

The wilderness, combined with the loneliness and desolation was indescribable. Flora felt like she was in another world. "Suspicion," she later wrote when she described this visit, "is heavy in the air. Outwardly, Afghanistan is a country of terrible barrenness. Inwardly, its people have an appalling need for

Christ, the only one who can give freedom, justice, and peace.''

After her Afghanistan visit, Flora sent her praying friends a picture of the old wall, which used to surround Kabul. It was now crumbling. Through a gaping crack in the wall one could see the mountain range behind. Underneath she had written the words, ''By faith, the walls of Jericho fell down!''

Although the walls around Afghanistan had not yet fallen, Flora had seen a crack in the wall. During her work in Asia she was frequently inspired by a poem of Anna Shipton's:

Sow ye beside all waters; ye shall reap if ye be not weary,
Sow though the thorns may wound thee; one wore the thorns
    for thee.
Sow, though the rock repeal thee, in its cold and sterile pride;
Some cleft there may be riven, where the little seed may hide.
Will Jesus chide thy weakness, or call thy labor vain?
On, with thy heart in heaven, thy strength—thy Master's
    might,
Till the wild waste places blossom in the warmth of the
    Saviour's light.[9]

11

A Crack in the Back Door

"God has said, 'Start moving so I may start blessing!' " [*az ou kas bitars tki as xuda nanetarsa!*]

Afghan proverb

"No land is closed to God. If we look around us, we will see that even if the front door is shut, a back door may be open."[1]

Mildred Cable, missionary to the Gobi desert region of central Asia, uttered these words in 1946. How right she was. Even though "missionaries" found Afghanistan's front door shut, the back door wasn't. One by one God began sending Christian professionals to have an influence for Christ throughout the country. Doctors, engineers, teachers—modern-day "tentmakers" following in the footsteps of the Apostle Paul— committed to Christian service.

In 1 Corinthians 9:1-23, Paul was accused of not being a bona fide apostle or missionary because he worked as a tentmaker and was self-supporting. Paul answered that he could have received support from the churches, as had other apostles like the brothers of Jesus and Peter; but he had chosen to be self-supporting to make the gospel free so he could "win the more" for Christ.

He testified to the Ephesian elders: "You yourselves know that these hands ministered to my own needs and to the men who were with me" (Acts 20:34).

He also explained his position to the Thessalonian Christians: "Nor did we eat anyone's bread without paying for it, but with labor and hardship we kept working night and day so that we might not be a burden to any of you; not because we do not have the right to this, but in order to offer ourselves as a model for you, that you might follow our example" (2 Thess. 3:8,9).

"Tentmakers" have played a significant role in shaping modern history. Marco Polo and Christopher Columbus attempted to evangelize the people they encountered on their journeys, even though their knowledge of how to go about doing it was very limited. William Carey supported himself and others in his India mission by operating an indigo factory. He also was a salaried professor of Sanskrit at the University of Calcutta. He wrote, "We have ever held it to be an essential principle in the conduct of missions that, whenever it is practicable, missionaries should support themselves in whole or in part through their own exertions."[2]

Henry Martyn (see chapter 9) was not allowed to go to India as a missionary in the early 1800s, so he went out as a chaplain for the East India Company. Robert Morrison, who translated the Bible into Chinese, supported himself by being an interpreter for a trading company. Explorer and missionary David Livingstone became a consul for the British government in Africa in the mid-nineteenth century. Pictures often show him wearing the hat of his office.

Christians, however, are not the only people to have proselytized by employing the "tentmaking" method of self-support. Muslims have spread Islam primarily through their traders and government administrators. Today Muslim adherents number over 750 million—more than twice the population of North America. Mormon and Jehovah Witness lay missionaries by the thousands have also spread their beliefs throughout the world. If the word of our Lord is to be proclaimed, Christians must take advantage of every opportunity to use their talents in other countries and cultures.

More and more governments around the world are hesitant to allow Christian "missionaries" into their country. But offer professional experience which can help the people of that nation, and your chances of obtaining a visa greatly increase—even in nations that are openly hostile to Christianity. If Christians do not fill foreign job opportunities around the world, not only will fewer people in those nations come to know Christ, others will go who could damage God's work.

Providentially, there were a few dedicated Christian professionals, "tentmakers," who took advantage of the rare opportunities to get into Afghanistan during the first half of this century. One of these Christian servants was Dr. Nazir Ullah. As a boy, he was kidnapped from his Nuristan home (eastern Afghanistan province) by cattle raiders. Taken to Peshawar, he was abandoned on the streets, and eventually raised by missionaries. He became a Christian and studied medicine under the influence of his foster family. On finishing his medical requirements, he worked for several years as house surgeon in a Peshawar hospital.

But early in 1913, the young Dr. Nazir Ullah was invited by some travelers to journey back over the Khyber Pass and visit his boyhood home. He accepted their invitation, and in the spring of that same year, went back to that remote section of Afghanistan. He was able to minister and witness for four months while he practiced his medical skills.

During the next decade, the opportunities began to open up for medical professionals to visit Afghanistan. Doctor and Mrs. Rolla Hoffman and Rev. and Mrs. Dwight Donaldson were working in Mashad, Iran, when permission was granted by the Afghan authorities for them to spend a couple of weeks in Herat. The time was spring, 1924.

"We felt almost as though we were on forbidden soil," wrote Mrs. Donaldson in *Prairie Girl in India and Iran,* "yet experienced a thrill that at least we were in Afghanistan!"[3] Hundreds of patients were examined and treated at the temporary dispensary. Reverend Donaldson controlled the tremendous crowds, while the two women helped Dr. Hoffman with the medical ministry.

Nine years later, in 1933, an American petroleum engineer was invited to investigate oil seepages near Herat. He took Rev. J. Mark Irwin with him as an interpreter. Reverend Irwin was able to talk with Muslim religious leaders about Christ and presented them with copies of the New Testament in Persian. As they took the books, the *mullahs* kissed the Scriptures to show their respect for God's Word.

In 1937, Professor Arthur Pope, an orientalist from the University of Chicago, Dr. Donald Wilber from the Princeton Institute for Advanced Study, and my father, Dr. J. Christy Wilson, a Presbyterian missionary in northwestern Iran, conducted an archaeological survey in western Afghanistan. My father was writing a book on the archaeology, art, and architecture of the area.[4] The men were able to examine ancient monuments in and around Herat, and were welcomed by the local officials and people.

There was another man who was *not* welcomed by the Afghan officials. His story is one of the most interesting of all the early "tentmakers" who had the rare privilege of being able to spend time inside Afghanistan's borders.

Dennis Clark, a young British businessman, visited Peshawar in the winter of 1943 in an effort to obtain ideas for getting the gospel message into the "closed" areas of central Asia. He saw that Peshawar was a great trade center, and realized that if he located a business there, he could minister to thousands of merchants who came to its bazaars from lands where no missionary could enter. The next fall his wife Gladys came to Peshawar. Each day Dennis talked to traders traveling between "closed lands" and India. He discovered that by wearing Pathan tribal clothes, he often passed as one of the people, and was able to get to know the traders in the bazaars.

"I began to conceive a plan by which I could become one of them as a merchant,"[5] he said. In April of 1944, he established the Central Asian Trading Agency, and decided with his wife that they would not take any profits out of the business for themselves. Dennis secured an office right in the heart of Peshawar, opposite the *serais* (business compounds) from which trade left for Kabul and other parts of central Asia. So began the Phillips Bicycle Concession. Miss Flora Davidson contributed the first 3,000 rupees to help get the business operating.

But the Clarks had a very difficult time. Dennis came down with typhoid fever, followed by pneumonia and a serious case of heat stroke. Then his business partner, an Indian who had claimed to be a Christian, embezzled much of the money and fled to Lahore. It took months for the Clarks to recover from the shock of their friend's unfaithfulness.

Officials also sought to discourage Dennis. Time and time again he was told he would never be granted permission to enter Afghanistan. One high-ranking intelligence officer told him confidentially that the Afghanistan government would most certainly not allow him to enter the country, since they knew too much about him. Most of his missionary friends thought that the project was impractical and a waste of time and money. To make matters worse, close British Central Intelligence Department C.I.D.) surveillance was placed upon him, and the Clarks' private correspondence was censored.

Before he could apply to the Afghanistan government to enter the country, he had to secure permission from the British to leave India. But the authorities there refused to grant him an exit permit on the grounds that "Mr. Clark's plea of business was only a cover for missionary activities."

Dennis Clark countered in a letter to the under secretary of the India government on August 8, 1944: "The ban is not on Christians, but on missionaries. I only ask for those facilities to cross borders that are accorded to subjects of all civilized powers irrespective of their religion."

Finally as he was about to give up hope, the answer came. "If you agree to the Afghan government being informed of your religious views, the government of India has no objection to granting you a passport for Afghanistan."[6] He agreed to this, and received his exit authorization.

But Dennis Clark's battle with red tape was only half over. He still needed an Afghan visa.

While he was waiting for permission to proceed to Afghanistan, he was able to make a trip into the closed areas of Chitral and Gilgit north-northeast of Peshawar as a trader. There he distributed Scriptures and witnessed for Christ. The British political agent in Gilgit angrily abused him, threatened to put him in handcuffs, and send him back to Peshawar under arrest.

"Is it illegal to speak in the name of the Lord Jesus?"[7] Dennis asked quietly.

The political agent eventually calmed down, but the incident made Dennis realize that some government officials were so afraid of Christian work that they would go to any length to stop it.

When Dennis returned to Peshawar there was still no word.

He had written many letters to Afghan officials as well as their representatives in New Delhi. Finally, Dennis felt it was time to put out a fleece. He made a pact with the Lord. October 24, 1945 was set as a deadline for word on the Afghan visa. (October 24 was not only his birthday, but it had been almost two years since he had first tried to get into Afghanistan.) If visa news was negative, he had determined to close down his business and seek to serve the Lord in some other way.

October 24 arrived to find Dennis bedridden with a fever. He was sick and very disappointed. But before he regained enough strength to begin closing down his business, a letter arrived from the Afghan consul general, dated October 25, 1945. The message? "We have no objection to your Afghanistan visitation."

The Clarks were elated with the news and Dennis made his plans as soon as he was well. He had looked forward to the time he would enter Afghanistan for eleven years. In fact, he practically knew the Afghanistan map by heart. When the big day finally arrived, he set off from the Afghan consulate *serai* along with Afghan merchants and other travelers. As Dennis began his journey his wife and Flora Davidson closeted themselves in prayer.

At Jamrud, the first border checking post, all the passengers were thoroughly searched for contraband materials, and as fate would have it, most of them carried concealed articles. For example, two hundred pounds of nails were discovered under the seat of the bus. Only Dennis and a couple of others were cleared. The truck, however, was impounded at the police post, pending a court case. So Dennis and the others had to return to Peshawar for the night and try again.

When Dennis knocked at the door of his home, he interrupted his wife, Gladys, and Flora who were at that very moment engaged in earnest prayer for him. They, of course, thought he had already crossed the Afghanistan border and was on his way to Kabul. But the delay was only temporary.

The next morning Dennis set out again. This time he passed the customs check without difficulty, ascended through the Khyber Pass, and soon reached the border post at Torkham. After clearing further formalities, he and his fellow passengers began the one-hundred-and-fifty-mile trip from there to Kabul on the worst roads Dennis had ever seen—"a cross between a ploughed field and a stony riverbed."

He arrived in Kabul on the second day of his journey and checked in at the only hotel in town. Everyone was extremely courteous, and he soon picked up the polite Persian phrases of meeting and greeting (always accompanied with a bow as he placed his right hand over his heart). After his passport was examined and stamped, he was free to go about the bazaar, establishing business contacts.

During those first days he had intended to remain quiet about the Lord, thinking he would speak about Jesus slowly and cautiously until he was well-established in the trading community.

But the Word of God dispelled all doubt as to the course he should pursue. As he turned to his Bible he realized that incident after incident in the Book of Acts described the aggressive witness of the apostles, often resulting in persecution and their expulsion from a city.

"The Lord indicated to me that his followers would be hated for his sake and brought before kings and governors for a witness," he said. "I felt I could not keep quiet. . . . So I commenced to speak of my Lord at every opportunity knowing full well the implications in such a country."

The word was soon out that there was a "Christian in the city."

One student came to see him in his hotel room and asked why Christians called Jesus the Son of God. Dennis contacted another student whom he had previously met in Peshawar. After talking with him further the young man seemed to believe in Christ. He said, however, that if his decision were known, his life would be in danger. Nevertheless, the young man introduced a high-ranking government official's son to Dennis so he, too, could hear the gospel.

That was as far as the Afghan authorities were willing to let Dennis Clark go. On December 6, a young Afghan zealot came to his hotel room and forbade him to speak about religious matters. He also demanded that Dennis accompany him to the Afghan Foreign Office.

There the Director of Political Section, a powerful and feared official interrogated him as if he were a captured spy. "He fired questions at me without waiting for an answer,'' Dennis remembered. "Then he accused me of engaging in 'religious propaganda.' He asked me how I got my visa, and I soon realized that it was granted in error."

The director of politics had been under the mistaken impression that Dennis had a lot of religious literature with him. When Dennis finally convinced him that he had only the one Persian New Testament he had brought with him, the director confiscated the small book.

Next, the interrogating officer tried to get Dennis to guarantee in writing that he would not speak in Jesus' name while in Afghanistan. Dennis refused and substantiated the validity of the gospel by referring him to verses in the Persian New Testament. This seemed to arouse the director's ire all the more. Especially when Dennis Clark said that he must obey God rather than man.

Dennis knew that he could very well be spending the night in the Kabul city jail. But instead, the director of political section sent him back to the hotel. That evening two police officers came and took away his passport and shortly before midnight one of them returned with an order for Dennis to leave the country.

The next day Dennis reported the matter to the British legation in Kabul and learned that they had already been informed of this situation. They told him that the Afghan government was afraid a fanatic might kill him if he remained. He was put under police guard, and escorted in a lorry to the border at Torkham. There he was handed his passport and politely bidden adieu.

Back with his family and Miss Davidson in Peshawar, Dennis reflected on his Kabul visit. He concluded that his business venture had served its purpose, and that he should move on to other service.

In accordance with their agreement with the Lord, Dennis and Gladys used the profits from the Peshawar business venture to establish the Christian Publishing House in Lahore. Today, about four decades later, this publishing operation is still producing Christian literature to help those working with the Muslim people in that part of the world.

Dennis Clark had entered Afghanistan in 1945 through a crack in the back door. Someone had issued his visa by mistake.

But the attitudes of Afghan officials toward outsiders had changed rapidly after World War II. Afghanistan was about ready to open its front door to foreigners—people who could bring the gospel message in with them.

12
Catching Up with a Twentieth-Century World

"Forget the past, but prepare for the future." [*quzashtaraw salawawt o awyindaraw aiteeawt.*]

Afghan proverb

The opening Flora Davidson and her "rope holders" were praying for occurred in 1947. That year saw a drastic change in the whole course of history for the nations of central Asia, including Afghanistan. For over two centuries, the great land of India had been governed by the colonial system of the British Empire. However, Britain, weakened by World War II losses, had realized that holding its claim to the Indian subcontinent would be unfeasible.

Northwest India, primarily Muslim, demanded separation from the rest of the country, which was primarily Hindu. Britain acquiesced to Muslim demands, and boundaries were drawn dividing those provinces with a Muslim majority from provinces with a Hindu majority. Partition on August 15, 1947 saw the British crown grant independence to India, and the new nations of West Pakistan and East Pakistan (Bangladesh).

In an indirect way, partition had a major effect on Afghanistan's future.

Britain had viewed this nation as a buffer between its territories and Russia to the north. For decades, the policy of the

British Raj was to keep borders with Afghanistan closed (see chapter 9). This was fine with the independent Islamic government of Afghanistan—the less outside interference, the better.

There was one problem with this thinking. While Afghanistan was in isolation behind the mountains of central Asia, the rest of the world was rapidly keeping pace with the technological and educational advancements of the modern era. Afghanistan had become a lost nineteenth-century nation in a twentieth-century world. Its leaders knew it was time to come out of their shell, and look to outside help for the development of their country.

Educationally, Afghanistan found itself far behind many third-world nations. Its literacy rate of only 3 percent was one of the lowest in the world. One small university, and only a handful of secondary schools, left Afghanistan sorely lacking in intellectual and leadership talent. Most small towns and villages scattered throughout the country had no educational program at all. Those that did usually saw the local *mullah* teaching only a handful of selected boys to read, so they would one day be able to interpret the Koran.

Consequently, improvement of the country's antiquated educational system became a top priority for the government during the late forties, fifties, sixties, and seventies. Announcements were sent to American, British, French, and German educational institutions inviting teachers to apply for positions in Afghanistan. One of these was posted on a bulletin board at Columbia Teachers College in New York City. It was copied and circulated through the Inter-Varsity Christian Fellowship. Many dedicated educators applied, encouraged mainly through the energetic efforts of Dr. Ralph Winter, now director of the United States Center for World Mission in Pasadena, California.

Richard (Dick) and Betty Soderberg, in 1948, were the first evangelical Christian couple to go to Kabul to teach. They were followed by Bob Maston. Howard and Wieps Larsen arrived on March 20, 1949, with Cliff and Mary Jane Benton coming three months later. Their assignment was to teach at Habibia College, the oldest high school for boys in the country.

The stream of ''tentmakers'' allowed to enter and take up residence in Afghanistan had finally begun.

In 1951, the Afghan minister of education, Dr. Abdul Majid, invited world-renowned literacy expert, Dr. Frank Laubach, to compile primers in Afghanistan's Dari and Pushtu languages.

Pushtu, the language of the Pashtuns or Pathans, is one of the two most commonly spoken languages in Afghanistan. It is related to Persian, and like that tongue, belongs to the Indi-Iranic branch of the Indo-European language family. Dari, or "Persian of Afghanistan," is spoken primarily in the central and western part of the country. In writing, it is similar to the principal language used in Iran, although there are marked differences in the way the two are spoken.

Doctor Laubach's team for the Afghan government-sponsored project included his wife; his son, Dr. Robert Laubach; Phil Grey, an artist and graphic designer; and my father, Dr. J. Christy Wilson. My father served as interpreter for the team since he was familiar with Persian.

The Laubach team worked day and night at the Hotel Kabul for a week and a half to complete the first forty-eight page primer. Evening work brought with it an interesting problem. The light in the room was supposed to draw from 220 volts of power. However, the Kabul power plant was not equipped to supply Kabul's mushrooming electricity demands, and at times, power would drop to as low as 40 volts. The lone light bulb in the hotel room looked like a glowworm hanging in a small glass bowl.

But Dr. Laubach had a job to do, and he was determined to do it. He put his chair on a table in the center of the room, and continued working with the dim light bulb suspended between his head and his book.

Finally it was time to put the new primer to use. Greeting Dr. Laubach that first morning of class were fifty illiterate army draftees from mountain tribes in distant provinces. None had ever been taught to distinguish one letter from another. The young soldiers even had to be shown how to hold their books and how to turn the pages.

Forty local teachers observed the daily sessions in order to learn the Laubach literacy teaching methods. They sat there in amazement as the soldiers learned to read the entire forty-eight page primer in fourteen days! Before his death in 1970, Dr. Frank Laubach had worked with more than three hundred and fifty languages around the world. Over 100 million people have learned to read through this simple, yet effective system, still widely used today.

Doctor Laubach's method is so simple, it's profound. Each letter is associated with the first letter of an object that is familiar to the beginning reader. Students first begin reading words they use every day in their vocabulary, and then move on to rarer words. They are usually so excited when they discover they are actually reading and understanding the print, that they can't wait for the next lesson.

The literacy campaign in Afghanistan was such a success that, much to the amazement of the American charge d'affaires, Dr. Laubach was invited to have an audience with the king and was awarded the nation's highest decoration. This in some ways was ironic. Doctor Laubach and my father had paid a visit to the American embassy in Kabul shortly after their arrival. Not knowing that the men were official guests of the Afghanistan minister of education, the acting American ambassador had lashed out, "You two Protestant ministers! What are you doing here in Kabul? How did you get into Afghanistan?"

But Dr. Laubach was not the only Christian professional to influence education in Afghanistan; Dick Soderberg also played a key role in improving the Afghan educational system. Dick had left an instructional position at the University of Southern California School of Engineering to teach in Afghanistan. Dick and his wife Betty saw a tremendous need for the establishment of a technical school. He drew up plans with the Afghanistan Ministry of Education, and on July 31, 1948, he signed a contract with the Afghan government.

He left for the United States at once to organize the program, recruit the faculty, secure equipment, and build an engineering library. Dick Soderberg agreed to return to Afghanistan with the personnel and equipment in early 1951. The Afghan government's part of the bargain was to provide the land for the campus and to put up new buildings for the institute.

With the assistance of Christian friends, he set up a nonprofit corporation called the Afghan Institute of Technology Incorporated (AITI). It was approved and registered in the State of California in June, 1949. Hugo H. Winter, father of Ralph Winter, accepted the position as president of the board of directors. At that time Hugo Winter was an engineer working for the City of Los Angeles, and he played a key role in the planning of the Los Angeles freeway system.

Dick Soderberg was named general director. An advisory council included professors from leading engineering institutions across the country. New Jersey lawyer Jacob Stam drew up a formal contract to be entered into jointly by the Afghan government and the newly formed AITI.

A *New York Times* article (May 24, 1949) resulted in several good recruiting leads. The story outlined Dick Soderberg's project and told of available teaching opportunities in Afghanistan.

By early 1950, Dick had lined up most of the faculty and had received contributions of books and equipment worth several thousand dollars. However, delicate negotiations still had to be completed in Kabul, so prospective faculty members and friends held a special day of intercessory prayer in Princeton, New Jersey, on October 21, 1950.

God answered their prayers. The Afghan government granted Dick Soderberg an air ticket so he could return to Kabul and hammer out more details on the project. Right on schedule, a new contract between AITI and the Afghan government was signed in Kabul on January 23, 1951, and classes convened the next fall.

Starting an educational institution in Afghanistan was no easy matter, but AITI was a success from the start. The faculty was made up primarily of Christians who were well-qualified in their respective fields. Many institute students went on to universities and vocational training institutions abroad. Others took up responsible positions in the life of their country. In fact, the Afghan Institute of Technology story was told in numerous publications, including *Reader's Digest Magazine*.

In order to establish similar projects in other developing countries, AITI was superceded in 1952 by a new nonprofit corporation, the International Technical Assistance Foundation (ITAF). Dick Soderberg resigned as principal of the Afghan Institute of Technology in 1953, in order to expand the work as ITAF general director. Paul Winter, brother of Ralph and son of Hugo, became the new head of AITI and served in that position until his contract expired in 1954. He was succeeded by Ed

Maguire, a Canadian educator.

About that time, the American government had begun to feel uneasy about the number of evangelical Christians that were now living and working in Afghanistan. One U.S. embassy official said, "The Christians at AITI are potentially a more dangerous threat here than the Russian Communists!"

The policy of the U.S. State Department was to support the religious status quo of Islam in every possible way. Our government reasoned that the atheistic Communists would have a difficult time forcing their will on strongly theistic Muslims. Not wanting to "rock the boat" in any way, the State Department feared that Christian "missionaries" from the United States would be viewed as a threat to Islamic nations. Consequently, the State Department attempted to thwart the efforts of Christians whenever possible.

So was the fate of the Afghan Institute of Technology. The U.S. government told the Afghans that the United States would take over the entire financial responsibility for the institute if the Afghans would cancel their contract with ITAF and sign a new one with the University of Wyoming. Beginning in 1955, teachers were hired by the University of Wyoming and were technically employees of that institution. The following religious clause appeared in the new contract:

> Employees are not to engage in religious proselytizing among citizens of Afghanistan and are to conduct themselves at all times in such a way as to reflect credit on the United States. The University will terminate the employment of any individual when it has been proved that such action is justified and necessary because of religious proselytizing. In the event of such termination the employee shall pay the cost of returning himself and family to the United States.[1]

When one teacher questioned the constitutionality of this in light of the basic freedoms guaranteed by the Bill of Rights, a University of Wyoming official replied that it had been inserted at the insistence of the U.S. State Department. Also, the director of the American Aid Program, openly announced after the takeover, "No more fundamentalists will be hired!"

Gradually, all the Christian teachers at AITI were released. Some returned to the States, but many were able to join other projects and stay in the country.

Afghan schools were not the only place United States diplomats made things difficult for Christian teachers. They also attempted to dictate policy at the English-speaking Christian schools for international children.

As the international population rose in the late forties and early fifties, it soon became evident that special educational facilities would be needed for children in the foreign community. For example, shortly after our arrival in 1951, my wife, Betty, was asked to start a kindergarten. That first year she taught seven boys and girls.

Over the years, as more children arrived with their families, attempts were made to continue Christian-oriented education for them. This desire, shared by several dozen parents, became a reality in January, 1958. That was when a Christian school was established.

Its first principal, Eva Ahlman, soon had to resign because of a bout with cancer and Maynard and Shirley Eyestone took over the administration at that point. When Eva Ahlman died, the school was renamed the Ahlman Academy in her honor, and was christened with the motto, ''Reverence for the Lord is the beginning of wisdom'' (Prov. 9: 10). The Bible was taught in all grade levels and classes were opened with prayer.

Members of the Yugoslavian Embassy once withdrew their children because of the Bible study requirement. However, one of their girls cried so much, she was given special permission by the ambassador to return.

Another student from a Communist country once told his teacher: ''There can't be a God or life after death, because no one had come back from the dead to tell us about it.''

''But someone has come back to tell us,'' his teacher responded.

''Who was that?'' the boy asked.

''The Lord Jesus Christ,'' she explained. ''He was crucified for our sins, rose from the dead three days later, and not only told us there was life after death, but proved it by rising from the dead himself.''

A smile came over the boy's face as he said, ''I'm so glad to hear you say that. My grandmother in Bulgaria has told me the same story.''

Not only were the children learning about Jesus, they were

receiving a quality education in other subjects as well. In 1964, four educators were sent by the State Department to evaluate overseas schools. They lauded upon Ahlman Academy high commendations as the most outstanding institution they had visited.

That same year Ambassador J.S. of the American embassy wanted to start another international school. That's when the real trouble started. He had hoped Ahlman Academy would amalgamate with the new institution. However, the issue was a little more complicated than the ambassador had envisioned. Many parents and Ahlman board members could see the benefits of a new American-government-sponsored international school. But the consensus was overwhelming that Ahlman should continue its operation. If Ahlman merged there would no longer be freedom to teach the Bible and have prayer in the classroom.

Ahlman board chairman, Dr. Rex Blumhagen, served as medical attache to the American embassy. Doctor Blumhagen defied the ambassador's order to close the academy, believing his loyalty to God came first. That stand on principle cost him his job, as he and his wife, Dr. Jeanne Blumhagen, were sent back to the States.

Norman Friberg, a Kandahar teacher, objected to this high-handed action. He and his wife were also sent home at the ambassador's request. Jim Cudney, American embassy media director, was transferred to another country. His crime was simply the fact that he happened to be married to an Ahlman Academy board member.

But J.S. still wasn't through. He also refused to allow any embassy parents to get educational allowances if they continued sending their children to Ahlman Academy. Consequently, several families paid all the tuition themselves since they wanted their boys and girls to get a Christian education.

In spite of the difficult circumstances, Ahlman Academy opened its doors again in September, 1964. Enrollment dropped from ninety to twenty-six children, but within one year, it was back up to ninety again. The school continued its vital ministry until its closure in 1980 following the Russian invasion.

Personally, I was involved in some aspect of education throughout my twenty-two years in Afghanistan. The Ahlman controversy occupied my attention as parent and pastor. Blind Institute classes were held in my home and I was married to a faculty member (see chapter 6). But my fondest memories come from my early years in Afghanistan when I taught at Habibia College, and tutored some very special people in their English lessons.

Habibia principal, Howard Larsen, went home on leave in 1954, and asked me to serve as acting principal. Governmental order could stop me from verbally sharing my testimony, but no governmental order can stop a person from living a Christian life before the students he comes to know and love. My witness to the students included being their friend and helping when they had a problem.

One of my students had just graduated from Habibia with high honors, and had won a United Nations scholarship to study petroleum engineering at the University of Texas. The day before he was to leave, he received news that he would first have to get a new registration paper. But when he applied for this, he was put off by the authorities. His problem was totally beyond his control. He was being discriminated against because he happened to be born an Uzbeki, one of Afghanistan's smaller tribes.

The next day, he brought me to the offices with him. But the answer was the same. One of the officials took me aside and told me that I was wasting my time trying to help him. The decision had already been made.

We didn't give up though. I appealed to the resident United Nations representative, since it was clearly a case of prejudice against the Uzbeki minority. He in turn told the prime minister that if Afghanistan did not accept this scholarship, it would be given to a Pakistani instead. The message had gotten through. Our honor student was immediately allowed to leave for Texas and following his education, he returned to Afghanistan to head up the natural gas project for the whole country.

Shortly after I arrived in Afghanistan, I had a very special opportunity. Howard Larsen had been tutoring the Crown Prince Ahmad Shah in English. He asked me to take over this instruction and two times each week I went to the royal residence for our lesson. Each session, the prince would excuse himself to go through the Muslim prayer, and while he was doing this, I also prayed silently.

Along with my other responsibilities, I was asked in March, 1954, to teach a special English course to members of the Afghan Ministry of Foreign Affairs. I continued this class for seven years, and it enabled me to get to know personally many of the future government leaders, including Noor Ahmad Etimadi, who later served as Afghanistan's prime minister in 1971 and 1972.

My friendship with many of Afghanistan's foreign diplomats helped on many occasions through the years. One incident particularly stands out in my mind. I had spent several months vacationing in the States with my family in 1965. I stopped at the Afghan embassy in Washington to get our visas renewed and was surprised when a young diplomat produced a copy of a recent newspaper article detailing one of my speeches. I had spoken at a large church and had reported on how God was using American Christians in the Peace Corps. (Afghan officials subscribed to a clipping service and had access to almost every article or notice published in the U.S. about Afghanistan.)

The young diplomat interrogated me about what I had said in that church and he seemed reluctant to renew our visas. I did some quick thinking and asked to see a senior official. I was in luck. Four other Afghan officials stationed at the embassy had studied English in my classes. When they learned that he had been questioning their friend, they all but told him to "jump in the Potomac." They ordered him to issue the visas immediately.

The friendship God had allowed me to develop with Afghan nationals had made it possible to bypass Afghanistan's rules and regulations and once again enter the country. Through the past few decades, God has used the friendships of many other dedicated Christian servants for his purposes as well.

13
A Helping Hand

"A real friend is one who takes your hand in time of sadness and weariness." [*dost awn as(t) ki geerad dasti dost dar piraishawn (h) awlee o darmawndagee.*]

Afghan proverb

One certain way to gain someone's respect and friendship is to lend a helping hand. Christian educators had answered Afghanistan's call for assistance in improving its educational system. But the wall of isolationism Afghanistan had placed around its borders had left the country in desperate need for technological help as well. When that wall was taken down, just as the teaching "tentmakers" had, a wave of Christian doctors, engineers, and agricultural experts showed God's love to the Afghan people by offering their professional know-how.

One man in particular had a significant role in helping to modernize some of Afghanistan's agricultural methods. His name was Dr. Kinston Keh, a small man in stature, but a giant of a man in spirit.

Raised in China, he was stationed in Afghanistan by the United Nations Food and Agricultural Organization. He had graduated from Peking University in 1913 and had moved on to study agriculture in France at the University of Toulouse, where he specialized in pisciculture and sericulture. Field projects saw him raise rainbow trout in the Pyrenees mountains and his research in sericulture included study at silkworm stations in southern France and northern Italy.

When Dr. Keh returned to China, he taught agriculture on the university level. One of his better students was a young man named Chou En-lai, who half a century later would become prime minister of the People's Republic of China. Doctor Keh was so impressed with the bright, young student that he helped the future Communist Party leader get a scholarship for agricultural studies in France. Unfortunately, that's not all Chou En-lai studied in Europe. It was there that he became a radical Communist.

In 1924 Dr. Keh was appointed as a member of the Governing Committee for Silk Production in China, headquartered in Shanghai. He organized a large farm near Chinkiang on the Shanghai-Nanking railway not far from the Yangtze River, which eventually produced 2 million grams of selected silkworm eggs. When the Japanese invaded China in the mid-1930s, he had to give up this plantation, and he moved to Yunnan where he started another sericultural farm near Chungking, the wartime capital of China.

Following the war, he returned to Nanking where he was elected general manager of the China Silk Company. But in 1949, he was forced to flee the country during the Communist takeover. Three years later, in May of 1952, he arrived in Kabul as adviser of sericulture with the United Nations. So effective were his methods, he almost single-handedly revolutionized silk production in Afghanistan.

Until Dr. Keh arrived, silkworm eggs had only been hatched in the spring. But by introducing modern scientific methods for hatching eggs, he was able to produce silk in the autumn as well, enabling farmers to have two crops each year. When he came to Afghanistan, the country was importing up to $30,000 worth of silkworm eggs a year from Russia, France, and Italy. Doctor Keh was able to introduce hybrid strains, which produced twice as much silk per cocoon as the imported varieties. He also introduced special mulberry tree seedlings, which were flown in from Japan and from which innumerable grafts were made onto local varieties.

By improving silkworm production, Afghan farmers found that they could increase their income from their land as much as twenty to fifty times. This meant that they could make better profits from silk than from raising opium, so many of them stopped their poppy production and raised mulberry trees and silkworms instead.

Doctor Keh believed that farmers needed more than just good advice or know-how; they needed practical help, or "show how." For this reason he worked right along with the people themselves instead of simply writing reports about what should be done.

One of the reasons why Dr. Keh worked so hard to help the people was because of a Bible story he had read. Doctor Keh had been touched by the story of Christ feeding the five thousand with two fish and five loaves of bread.

Just as Christ felt compassion for the hungry multitudes, Dr. Keh was committed to helping Afghanistan increase food production. He knew he didn't have the faith to take two fish and multiply them five thousand times, but he did know a great deal about raising fish. Consequently, he offered to head up a special piscicultural project in addition to his regular sericultural work with the United Nations.

Most of the fish in the rivers, streams, and mountain lakes of Afghanistan were of the foul-tasting, bony-carp family. There were no rainbow trout. The New York State Conservation Department was contacted, and 25,000 rainbow trout eggs were contributed. These were flown to Afghanistan packed in ice, and arrived in the middle of November, 1956. Under Dr. Keh's supervision, a fish hatchery had been built in the Paghman mountains, northwest of Kabul. The trout eggs hatched, but the weather that winter was so cold that none of the small fish survived. There is a saying that goes, "If you fail once, try and try again." And so another shipment was ordered, this time from Japan. These eggs hatched, and were released as fingerlings in the streams and lakes of Afghanistan.

Later, King Zahir Shah was out fishing with one of his sons when the boy hooked a large rainbow trout. The fish gave the young sportsman a good fight, and of course, the meat of the boneless filet had a delicious flavor after it simmered over the charcoal fire.

The king enjoyed it so much that he ordered the Ministry of Agriculture to expand pisciculture. From this small beginning, there developed an extensive program of hatcheries, stream stocking, and fish production in Afghanistan.

The king was intrigued when he heard how Dr. Keh had stocked the waterways with rainbow trout and asked if there was also a possibility of securing Long Island ducklings. (Long Island ducklings originally were known as the Peking duck, which missionaries had brought from China to North America.)

Mr. and Mrs. Robert Goff, friends of mine from Long Island, responded to our "SOS" and sent forty-eight eggs by air. But the eggs were delayed at the Karachi Airport and didn't arrive for almost three weeks. To make matters worse, it was the hottest time of the year.

It seemed impossible that any would hatch after this harsh treatment. But believing in the God of miracles, Dr. Keh gave twenty-four to the Ministry of Agriculture to be placed in an incubator. The other twenty-four were put under setting hens.

Prayer was offered to the Lord that at least one pair would hatch, which was all, according to Dr. Keh, that would be needed. Jubilation filled the air when hatching day arrived! The incubator produced one duckling and the setting hens hatched two! One of these fledglings was a duck and two were drakes. They were taken to the king's farm north of Kabul where the one duck laid over eighty eggs that first season. The king was so involved with this project that he numbered and autographed each one so that none would be stolen.

Today these ducks are found throughout Afghanistan. They forage in the irrigation ditches, and provide a reasonable source of nourishment for the people. Their feathers provide down for quilts, and warm clothing in the cold weather.

But their most important benefit is something that no one even thought of. Afghanistan's principal source of income has been from sheep. Wool is made into beautiful carpets, piece goods, or exported in bales. Karakul lamb furs bring millions of dollars into the country each year. The sheep also provide other valuable export items such as sausage casings.

There is a problem, however. A liver-fluke disease kills many of these animals. Its parasite is transmitted by a snail. From this host it is deposited on the grass, is then ingested by the sheep, and then attacks the liver. Diseased sheep infect other snails with the parasite, and so the damaging cycle continues. The ducklings, however, eat the snails and are not adversely affected by them. Thus they break the life cycle of the liver fluke, and are helping to bring this disease under control.

Why did Dr. Kinston Keh have such a service-minded attitude? Doctor Keh's mother had become ill while he was in his formative boyhood years. She had received treatment at the nearby China Inland Mission hospital and had sensed there was something different about the staff members. There, she was told about the Lord Jesus Christ, and accepted him as her Savior. She recovered and returned home, where she shared her faith with her husband, and finally he believed, too.

Doctor Keh's parents both died when he was studying in France, but he never forgot their Christian example. Later, he decided that he, too, would become a Christian, and he received instruction in the faith and was baptized.

Doctor Keh moved to Japan, Brazil, and finally to the States when he retired. But the rainbow trout, the Long Island ducklings, the silkworms, and mulberry trees remain in Afghanistan as evidence of his Christian love in action.

Many other people and organizations have played a part in helping Afghanistan with its nourishment needs.

The years of 1956 and 1957 brought drought to the highlands of central Asia. During the cold winter of 1957, the price of bread began to soar, making it difficult for many families to afford nutritious food with their meager incomes. American wheat was brought in along with tons of white cake flour, since it was believed that this would keep better for a longer period of time. As a result, people shopping in the bazaars began to purchase white bread in large quantities, instead of the usual brown whole wheat "nan" bread (baked in the shape of large snowshoes). Brown bread was more nourishing. But the imported wheat and flour brought the price of bread down, for which the people were very grateful. Many Afghans told me, "When we were hungry, the people of America fed us."

Since no relief organizations operated in the country at that time, the Kabul Community Christian Church wrote to CARE, headquartered in the United States to see if it could extend its aid to Afghanistan. In due time CARE responded. Their first project was to bring powdered milk into the country so that students in the government schools, most of whom were suffering from malnutrition, could have this supplement in their diet.

However, rumor spread that it was pig's milk. People said a cow never gave milk in powdered form! Many students refused to drink it, even though it was reconstituted in liquid form for them. Today, powdered milk is still available in Afghanistan and is appreciated.

Northwest of Kabul, there was a poor farm—home for about four hundred people who had no other means of subsistence. Living there were orphans and widows as well as the blind, lame, insane, and those suffering from leprosy. The poor farm was also a way the municipality controlled excessive begging. Except for religious begging, which was allowed on Thursdays, beggars caught on the streets were sent to the farm.

Moved by the desperate plight of these people, the church collected clothing, shoes, toys, and food from people in the international community and distributed the goods. Money was contributed for this project, and secondhand clothing was bought, which had been collected by the Salvation Army and rescue missions in the United States and shipped in bundles to the bazaars of Asia. The church was able to purchase warm overcoats for about two dollars each.

This charity, however, was misunderstood by some. The head of the poor farm thought we were doing it in order to earn our salvation (see chapter 3). We tried to explain that we did this because we loved the people living there. God had already given us salvation freely in Christ, we said, and by helping others we could show our love and gratitude to him.

There were also tremendous medical needs at the poor farm. For example, those with leprosy were being allowed to rot away. The Community Christian Church was able to secure medicine for them to take, which could arrest the disease. Artificial arms were also ordered from abroad for two men who had families to support.

The need for doctors in Afghanistan was extremely great. Doctors were so few and far between, members of the international community often had to go untreated in a time of real crisis. Deaths occurred that could have been avoided with proper care. Best-selling author James Michener was in Afghanistan in the mid-1950s collecting material for his book, *Caravans*. His host, Dr. Harold Amoss, head of the Asia Foundation, came down with a serious illness. Michener tried his best to get adequate medical help, but couldn't, and therefore he had to do his best for Amoss himself. Following this experience, Michener wrote letters to the *New York Times* charging the U.S. State Department with negligence in sending its people to a place like Afghanistan without providing adequate health care.

The negative publicity worked. It wasn't very long before the arrival of the first State Department M.D., Dr. John Wilson. A graduate of Moody Bible Institute, he and his wife, Alice, who was a nurse, soon set up a small but well-equipped dispensary.

Doctor and Mrs. Wilson left after a two-year tour of duty, and they were replaced by Dr. Rex Blumhagen and his wife, Dr. Jeanne Blumhagen. Their arrival in Afghanistan fulfilled the Blumhagens' dream of twenty-three years. They had felt God's call to Afghanistan so strongly, that they had originally applied to come to Afghanistan as chemistry teachers, even though they were both medical doctors. But each time, something came up to stop them from going. It meant, however, that they were able to get further medical experience in Kentucky, Alaska, and California.

When the Blumhagens came to Kabul that November of 1960, there was a high incidence of hepatitis in the American community. They had gamma globulin flown in from Europe and injected all U.S. citizens. They also found many persons plagued with amoebic dysentery. Their investigation revealed that those who were preparing the Americans' food were carrying the infection, so the Blumhagens started a hygienic course for cooks. Even chefs from the local hotels attended the sessions.

Tests showed that all of the first group to attend had amoebic infections themselves. Since some Afghans thought that germs were just a superstition, the Blumhagens used a microscope to show them the germs that came from their own hands. After taking the course, one cook scrubbed up like a surgeon before preparing any meals.

Once a little American girl was born prematurely and began to have complications, because of an Rh-negative blood factor. With no blood bank available, the Blumhagens had to use live donors who were Rh-negative type O. The baby had to be given four total blood changes. The two doctors had no sleep for forty-eight hours as they labored to save the infant.

On another occasion, the queen's sister gave birth to a premature baby who was born in the sixth month and weighed only a little over two pounds. The Blumhagens said the only chance for the little girl to live was if she had constant and excellent nursing.

Shortly before this, Miss Ellen Rasmussen, a Danish missionary nurse, had been led to come to Kabul after her retirement from thirty-five years of service in mission hospitals on the Afghan borders (see chapter 10). She was eminently qualified to care for the baby. At first, a feeding was required every two hours. Since the baby was too young to suck, she had to be fed through a tube in her nose. Ellen Rasmussen could not get more than one hour of sleep at a time as she nursed the child night and day.

To avoid infection, the Blumhagens ordered a ban on all visitors except the parents. Once the king came to call wanting to see his new niece. But Ellen, faithful to her orders, would not let him in. The little girl won her struggle for life, and Ellen continued to care for her for several years, living in the home of the queen's sister.

A Christian in Afghanistan's royal palace? With God, all things are possible.

In recognition of her dedicated service to the royal family in Afghanistan, the king of Denmark presented Ellen with a gold medal on her seventieth birthday, September 20, 1969.

Other Christian doctors also came to Afghanistan under the sponsorship of MEDICO, a small organization specializing in supplying medical service to people throughout Asia. One of these men was Dr. Robert Shaw, who had been challenged by a statement his father, a Methodist minister, had made years earlier: "What the world needs today is dedicated Christian laymen."

"Although I still believe that being a minister or a missionary is the greatest calling," Dr. Shaw said, "I feel my father's statement was correct. Person-to-person contact in deeds of understanding is the manner in which Christian laymen can make their greatest impact. God has a job for every individual."

Doctor Shaw and his wife, a nurse, arrived in 1961. But that wasn't his first trip into Afghanistan. As a young man in 1929, he had driven over the rough road of the Khyber Pass. He had hoped to train to be a medical missionary, and work on the frontier of Afghanistan until he could get a visa to study in the country. However, in medical school he contracted pulmonary tuberculosis, which left a spot on his lung and disqualified him for acceptance with a mission. He specialized in thoracic surgery, and taught medicine in Dallas, Texas. As his career progressed, he still had hopes that he might one day serve in Afghanistan.

So when MEDICO invited him to head up their team in Kabul, he accepted, and went on to perform the first open-heart surgery in the country. After his first tour of service in Afghanistan, he returned to Dallas, and was working at Parkland Hospital when President John F. Kennedy and Texas Governor John Connally were shot. He was called in on the president's case, and was the surgeon in charge of Governor Connally's lifesaving operation. He also examined the corpse of alleged assassin, Lee Harvey Oswald.

Doctor and Mrs. Shaw returned to Afghanistan again in 1966, at which time he set up a special chest surgery unit adjacent to the Afghan government-operated Avicenna Hospital in Kabul. The medical equipment was brought by ship to Karachi, and then overland to Kabul by way of Quetta and Kandahar. The Shaws headed up this project until 1968, when they returned again to Dallas. In 1970, Dr. Shaw was asked by the Indiana University-Loma Linda Consortium to be a professor in the Nangrahar University Medical School at Jalalabad, fifty miles west of the Khyber Pass. He and his wife completed their service in Afghanistan by assisting in this teaching project.

After CARE and MEDICO joined forces, another Christian, Dr. John Hankins, came to Kabul. John had become a Christian through the witness of some fellow students in college. At the end of medical school, he felt called to the foreign mission field and signed a decision card to that effect at a Christian student conference.

The army assigned him to Iran where he served in a small army hospital for nineteen months. There, he realized service to the people of Iran was to be his ''mission field,'' and he returned to the southern Iran town of Shiraz after his discharge. He had been able to learn Persian well enough to carry on limited conversation with patients. He often prayed with them and talked with them about the Lord.

"During this entire period," said Dr. Hankins, "I enjoyed rich fellowship and mutual encouragement with the national Christians and British missionaries associated with the local church in Iran.

"I learned about the work being done in Afghanistan by Christians who had gone there in secular jobs. I visited there in 1962, and the Lord seemed to indicate to me that this was where he would have me serve him after my furlough."

John Hankins returned to practice medicine in Afghanistan under a contract with no clause prohibiting him from engaging in Christian activities. He took full advantage of his freedom to share his faith. Those who seemed interested in knowing more about Jesus Christ were given Persian Scripture portions, which they took home with them.

"The five years in Afghanistan were perhaps the richest five years of my life," he wrote to a friend. "I regularly prayed with my patients."

One young cancer patient who Dr. Hankins took a special interest in, showed no response to Dr. Hankins's witness during his initial treatment. However, two years later he came back to the hospital when the cancer returned. He came to church, and was befriended and prayed for by many of the Christians there. Ultimately, he made a profession of faith in Christ—another Muslim convert saved because a Christian friend had lent a helping hand.

14
IAM

"Two are better than one, and three than two." [*az yakee kada doo khoob as(t) o az doo kata sai.*]

Afghan proverb

Teachers . . . Doctors . . . Engineers . . . Construction workers . . . Agronomists . . . Foreign diplomats . . . God's "tentmakers" had been represented in almost every occupation. As the calendar moved into the 1960s, the Afghan government had allowed non-Muslims more and more leeway to share their beliefs. Restrictions and regulations were still tight, but I could definitely notice the difference as my second decade of work in Afghanistan progressed.

Then, early in 1965, those of us in the Christian community saw a major breakthrough. Until then, no "official" missionary had been allowed into the country. People affiliated with mission agencies had been left to continue their work in the Afghan border regions of Pakistan and Iran. But at that time, the go-ahead was given to allow Christian missionaries to come in and assist with various professional needs. Approximately one dozen mission agencies had personnel working on the borders of Afghanistan, and the time seemed ripe for these mission organizations to pool their resources in a cooperative united fellowship rather than work as separate missions. One united agency would be less confusing and threatening to the Afghan authorities.

The trustees of the Kabul Community Christian Church extended invitations to these border missions to attend a conference and pray about the possibility of entering Afghanistan as a united fellowship. On August 17-19, 1965, representatives from the following ten missions met in Murree, Pakistan: the Afghan Border Crusade; the Bible and Medical Missionary Fellowship; the Brethren; the Church Missionary Society; the Danish Pathan Mission; the Finnish Lutheran Mission; The Evangelical Alliance Mission (TEAM); the United Presbyterian Commission; the World Mission Prayer League; and the Worldwide Evangelization Crusade.

The first day the delegates sought God's guidance through prayer, and began to hammer out the logistical details of such a merger. The constitution of the United Mission to Nepal was used as a basis for planning the work in Afghanistan, and was adapted to the situation there. By conference end, the International Afghan Mission (IAM) was unofficially well on its way to becoming a very effective outreach ministry.

The representatives scheduled their next meeting for Lahore, Pakistan, six months later. That way there would be time to incorporate input from the main offices of their respective organizations. However, late in 1965, the Seventeen-Day War between India and Pakistan raged near Lahore, and that city was not considered a safe meeting place.

India and Pakistan had been at odds over ownership of Kashmir ever since partition in 1947. Controlled by India, the Pakistanis felt that they should govern the province since it possessed a Muslim majority. (Feeling over Kashmir runs high in both India and Pakistan to this day, and fighting has broken out several times in the last three decades.)

Alternate arrangements were made and the representatives were invited to Kabul instead. Great care was exercised so as not to alarm the Afghan government, so each mission was asked to limit representation to one person.

Again the meetings started with a day of prayer and devotions. But this time the conference had its share of tense moments. The constitution of the United Mission to Nepal presented the main problem. It affirmed belief in ''the canonical

Scriptures of the Old Testament and the New Testament as the inspired Word of God.'' Several delegates had asked that ''infallible'' be inserted in front of the phrase ''inspired Word of God.'' Others felt it would be better to have a term that expressed the idea both biblically and positively.

Eventually, the decision was made (based upon 2 Timothy 3: 16 that ''all scripture is given by inspiration of God'') to insert the word ''fully.'' Everyone was satisfied and the representatives voted unanimously to approve the constitution and officially establish the International Afghan Mission. The IAM was not set up to be a new mission organization with an office abroad. It was simply a fellowship of workers on the field, depending on existing missionary agencies to recruit, send, and secure personnel for the work in Afghanistan. Each mission in turn was entitled to a position on the governing board.

Representatives decided to disassociate the term ''missionary'' from IAM use because of its political connotation. Afghans, with their Muslim background, had the mistaken idea that the missionaries on their borders were the religious arm of Western armies who would forcibly seek to convert people under their jurisdiction. Instead the word ''Christian'' doctors, nurses, secretaries, etc., was used to denote those associated with the International Afghan Mission.

The next month, a one-day conference of doctors and nurses was held at the Church Mission Society hospital in Peshawar. Afghanistan still had a great need for medical professionals and so plans were made for the IAM medical work.

Doctor Howard Harper was one of the first IAM doctors to get into the country. He was invited by CARE-MEDICO in September, 1965, to assist with eye work in Lashkar Gah. The United States Agency for International Development (USAID) had constructed a hospital for this new desert town, located on the banks of the Helmand River. The 200-bed medical facility had been staffed by Peace Corps nurses and CARE-MEDICO doctors. However, there was a problem. The multimillion dollar complex had been virtually sitting empty. Only a small percentage of the rooms were being occupied by the Afghan people at any one time.

Things changed quickly following Dr. Harper's arrival, as he performed more than two hundred eye operations. The hospital soon was full to overflowing for the first time. One USAID adviser mentioned that Dr. Harper's medical visit had produced the greatest positive impact he had seen in the program during the seven years he had been working there.

Late in 1965, the acting minister of health, Dr. Mohammed Anwari, invited Dr. Harper to visit his Kabul office. The Afghan official had just returned from India where he had visited mission hospitals. He had heard glowing reports about Dr. Harper's work with the United Christian Hospital in Lahore and had decided that Dr. Harper was the man to head ophthalmological efforts in Afghanistan. Could Dr. Harper recruit an eye team, which could do work in other places similar to that which had been done in Lashkar Gah, the health minister wanted to know.

Doctor Harper said he'd try and then mentioned a need for trachoma control, a central eye hospital, and an eye bank of corneal transplants.

Doctor Anwari replied, "Put your recommendations into writing so that I can present them to the Cabinet."

Harper agreed.

He and his family moved to Afghanistan at the end of January, 1966, and in the next three months he made fifty-seven visits to the Ministry of Health. As a result, the protocol agreement with the Afghan government for the National Organization of Ophthalmic Rehabilitation (NOOR), an arm of the International Afghan Mission (IAM), was signed in April of 1966.

The next year the Afghan government set aside seventeen acres of property in the Darul Aman area southwest of Kabul for an Ophthalmological Center. It was to include an eye hospital, the Institute for the Blind facility (see chapter 6), and an Optician Training Unit. The Ministry of Health insisted that the building for the Institute for the Blind be used first as a temporary eye hospital. So, the NOOR eye doctors and nurses moved into this building in July, 1970, and within a few days, every bed was occupied. The doctors were seeing over two hundred patients each day. The new eye hospital was under construction for most of 1971 and 1972, with major funds coming from Christians in Germany. It was opened in March of 1973.

Besides the ophthalmological program in Kabul, clinics were

held in many parts of the country where thousands of operations have been performed. Trachoma was a particular problem in Herat, and so a public-health eye team was established there.

The breakthrough for IAM doctors was most significant for Dr. Rex Blumhagen and his wife, Dr. Jeanne Blumhagen. The former State Department sponsored couple was able to return to Afghanistan in early March, 1966, under the commission of the Bible and Medical Mission Fellowship. Their assignment was to conduct a survey for the Medical Assistance Program (MAP International).

J.S. still served as American Ambassador, so the Blumhagens paid him a courtesy call when they arrived in Kabul. They told the ambassador that they realized he had done what he felt was best when he had dismissed them (see chapter 12). However, they now hoped the past would be forgotten.

The ambassador was so incensed by their return, that he sent a communication to the Afghan Ministry of Foreign Affairs, requesting that the Blumhagens' visa be revoked. Within a matter of hours passport officials ordered them to leave the country.

But God had called the Blumhagens to Afghanistan and they were determined to stay. Earnest prayer was offered throughout the international community on their behalf. It wasn't long before those prayers were to be answered. Jeanne Blumhagen was walking through downtown Kabul when she bumped into the wife of Deputy Prime Minister, Dr. Shahlezi. The Blumhagens had helped this family when they were embassy doctors, so Mrs. Shahlezi invited the Blumhagens to visit her husband.

The deputy prime minister greeted them with the words, "I am so glad you are back in our country. I need twenty-eight other foreign doctors like yourselves, one for each of the provinces outside the capital."

He added that with the new representative government, there was pressure to establish good medical services in the provinces. Unfortunately, he said, some of the local doctors were often more interested in their own remuneration rather than their opportunity to serve.

"We need doctors like you and Mrs. Blumhagen who demonstrate real compassion for their patients," the deputy prime minister added.

That was when Dr. Rex Blumhagen broke the news of what had happened.

Doctor Shahlezi was thrilled to be in a position to help and replied, "Come to my office, and I'll see that you get your visas."

Ambassador J.S.'s attempt to have the Blumhagens deported for the second time had failed. The ambassador had also attempted to stop a nationwide literacy program conducted by Dr. Frank Laubach. The literacy teacher had once again been invited back into the country by the Afghan government. So a concerned Dr. Laubach sent word to President Lyndon Johnson questioning the American ambassador's opposition to this unique opportunity to help the people of a strategically located country.

The president ordered an investigation, and as a result, Ambassador J.S. was transferred, leaving Afghanistan on July 21, 1966.

Meanwhile, the Blumhagens were asked to draw up a medical project for work in the provinces, and a second protocol agreement was signed in May, 1966, with the Afghan Ministry of Public Health for a Medical Assistance Program project. A new International Harvester bus was refitted as a mobile medical unit, and Dr. and Mrs. Blumhagen, along with Miss Ellen Rasmussen, began to make trips into the central highlands.

Thousands of Afghans, totally unfamiliar with the miracle of modern medicine, received medical attention for the first time. Some people didn't quite know what to make of it all. Once when Dr. Blumhagen gave antibiotic pills to a man who had an ear infection, he began stuffing them in his ear. The man had never seen pills before and didn't realize he was supposed to swallow them.

In the late 1960s, the Afghan Ministry of Health asked the Blumhagens to establish a medical center at Nyak, located in the Yakaolang Valley of the mountainous Hazarajat region. The center became home base, while the medical team set up outlying satellite stations.

Leprosy and tuberculosis were very common in this area, and in order to provide regular treatment for these patients, the MAP team spent the winter of 1969-70 in that high, mountainous region. The main part of the team was located at the Nyak station, however; two nurses, Pat Cook and Rosina Woodland, were in charge of the satellite station at Panjao. The two nurses were able to care for more than sixty patients a day. Difficult cases were referred to the doctors in Nyak over shortwave radio for diagnosis.

During the summer of 1970 many short-term workers were granted permission to enter the country and assist in the MAP program, and in May of 1971, a Missionary Aviation Fellowship plane, a Cessna-185, arrived to assist with the work in the mountains. Airstrips were built in various locations. During the winter weather when some satellite stations were isolated, the plane was able to fly personnel in and out, make mail drops, and serve as an ambulance for emergency cases that needed to be evacuated to Kabul. Under most circumstances, receiving permission to fly the plane in Afghanistan would have been next to impossible. But the president of the Afghan Air Authority, H.R.H. Sardar Sultan Ghazi, was more than happy to OK the request. The life of his premature daughter had been saved by the Blumhagens and Ellen Rasmussen some years before.

God had blessed the work of the International Afghan Mission in a mighty way. The first board meeting, in July, 1966, saw 9 workers from 6 different nations involved with the ministry. By early 1973, IAM had 119 members from 14 nations, representing 21 supporting agencies. But the IAM work had its setbacks, too.

The twilight of August 8, 1971 brought with it unusual beauty and a feeling of serenity over the Kabul Valley. Josephine White, a dedicated American medical technician drove into the foothills outside the city with her friend Susan Fry, an Australian occupational therapist. They had hoped to find a quiet spot to pray and watch the sun set over the western horizon. Little did Josephine realize that she would never return to tell about her evening.

While they were praying, two Afghan thieves approached the car. Jo started to drive away, but one of them drew his gun and demanded that she halt. She didn't. So he shot her through the open window of the car, killing her instantly.

Josephine White experienced a violent death because she refused to give up her money. However, many other committed Christian servants in Afghanistan have faced painful torture and death because they refused to give up something even more precious—their faith in Jesus Christ.

15
The Blood of Martyrs

"In childhood you are playful. In youth you are lustful. In old age you are feeble. So before God, when will you be worshipful?" [*dar kkurdee pastee, dar jawawnee mastee, dar peeree sustee, pas khudaurar kaee parastee?*]

An Afghan poetical proverb by Abdullah
Ansari of Herat

Islam's law of apostasy states that anyone leaving the Muslim faith should be killed (see chapter 3). In fact, Muslims are taught that anyone who executes an apostate assures the entrance of his victim and himself into paradise. Though this custom in the Islamic world is now a rarity, leaving Islam for Christianity is still a very dangerous move. Most Afghan Christians live under dogged persecution, which is why you will find few Christians with a lukewarm faith in Afghanistan. It's either all or nothing. The numbers who have given all—converts who have been beaten, tortured, and have died a martyr's death through the years, are many.

Yahya Baqui was a zealous Afghan Muslim from Kandahar. In 1855 he made the long pilgrimage to Mecca, but was warned in a dream that he should follow Christ. Not quite knowing what to make of it all, he met Dr. Karl Pfander during a layover in Peshawar on his way home. Doctor Pfander, a medical missionary, explained to *Hajji* Yahya Baqui the significance of his dream and baptized him as the first Afghan convert to Christ.

It wasn't long before the new convert's faith was put to the ultimate test. One night *Hajji* Yahya Baqui was attacked by some who were trying to carry out Islam's law of apostasy, and he was left for dead. Though he bled profusely from seven wounds, he miraculously recovered. Two of his fingers had been cut off and for the rest of his life, like the apostle Paul, he bore scars on his body. He returned to Afghanistan where he witnessed boldly for Christ and was wonderfully protected until he died a natural death.[1]

However, others did not meet with the same fortune as *Hajji* Yahya Baqui.

Dilawar Khan was another Afghan who had been led to Christ through the ministry of Dr. Pfander. He had been a notorious outlaw and border raider with a price on his head. On receiving Christ, he gave himself up and claimed his own reward! Then he joined the British Army in India and became a high officer. His characteristic bravery spilled over into his spiritual life and he did not hesitate to confess Christ publicly.

A military journey brought him to Kabul where he was recognized by an Afghan who had heard him preach in the Peshawar bazaar. Dilawar Khan was arrested and accused before a *qazi* (judge). A copy of a book given to him by Dr. Pfander was used as evidence against him.

The magistrate proceeded to tear the book in two and he condemned Dilawar Khan as an apostate, ordering that he be blown to his death at the mouth of a cannon. The king, however, heard of the case and asked to see the book. He inspected it, pronounced it a good book, and set Dilawar Khan at liberty. His freedom didn't last long though. He was sentenced to death by a treacherous ruler in the mountains of Chitral.[2]

Doctor Theodore Pennell, who started the hospital in Bannu, told the story of another Afghan convert in the early twentieth century. One of the merchants from Laghman in Afghanistan had taken his young son, Jahan Khan, with him to India on one of his journeys. The father was stricken with dysentery, and the boy took him to a mission hospital, where for the first time he heard the gospel story. At first Jahan Khan plugged his ears lest any of the words spoken by the mission doctor defile his faith.

The father, however, did not improve, and was taken to a shrine of a famous saint for healing. Instead, he died. His heartbroken son had to bury him near the saint's tomb. Consequently, Jahan Khan found himself an orphan hundreds of miles away from his family.

Doctor Pennell was looking for a servant who knew Pushtu so that he might gain proficiency in that language. Jahan Khan resented the idea of becoming a servant to an infidel, which he thought would jeopardize his Islamic salvation. The young boy only accepted the position after his Muslim patron had laughed at his scruples. "So long as you say your prayers regularly, read the Koran, keep the fast, and do not eat their food lest by any chance there should be swine's flesh in it, you have no reason to fear," the Muslim advised Jahan.

After he had worked at the hospital for a while, an educated Afghan twitted Jahan Khan about his inability to read. So the embarrassed boy persuaded the hospital *munshi* (secretary) to give him a lesson every day. Jahan Khan's first reading lessons came from a Pushtu Gospel, which riveted his attention. Instead of the law of "an eye for an eye and a tooth for a tooth," Jahan read about an incredible command that said to forgive your enemies.

Soon, Jahan Khan began to talk constantly about the gospel message, much to the chagrin of the local Muslims. One evening as Dr. Pennell was sitting in his room, he heard shouts from outside, *"O daktar Sahib! O daktar Sahib!"* Two Muslims had seized Jahan and were beating him, while they tried to stifle his cries by choking him with his turban. But Jahan's close call didn't deter him from reading and talking about Christ's teachings. Instead, he avowed himself publicly to be a Christian shortly after the attempted murder.

After his baptism, Jahan had a burning desire to visit his childhood home. His widowed mother was still living there with his brothers and cousins, and he wanted to tell them about his newfound faith. Doctor Pennell pointed out the great dangers that could confront him. Becoming a convert to Christianity was at that time a capital offense in Afghanistan. Jahan Khan, however, could not be dissuaded. Some Gospel copies in Dari and Pushtu were sewn inside his Afghan garment and off he went.

His mother and brothers received him with delight. But as soon as it was known that he was a Christian, the villagers clamored for his life. An uncle, who was himself a *mullah,* managed to appease the angry mob on condition that Jahan leave the country at once. He left his books with some *mullahs* and joined a caravan leaving Afghanistan through the Khyber Pass. But he still wasn't safe. Someone had mixed a poisonous herb in his soup.

Jahan Khan remembered nothing more until the caravan entered Peshawar. It was several days before he was able to make the journey on to Bannu, and still longer before he regained his previous health. But his visit had not been without fruit. A brother and two cousins journeyed down from Laghman to Bannu, and while there, one of them requested Christian baptism.

Jahan Khan eventually followed in Dr. Pennell's footsteps and became a doctor. Since there was such a great need for medical work in Karak, he and his devoted wife, who was also a Pathan Christian, started work there. Through their kindness to the sick and needy they served, the Khans overcame the local anti-Christian prejudice and antagonism. Dr. Pennell wrote, "I have no greater pleasure than to visit Karak and to see these two faithful workers in their hospital, surrounded by the sick and needy, telling them of the precious sacrifice of Christ."[3]

Sir Henry Holland, medical doctor in charge of the Quetta missionary hospital, told of another faithful Afghan convert who had a burning desire to preach the gospel in Afghanistan. Qazi Abdul Karim, the son of a Muslim judge, worked with the mission hospital in Quetta, and witnessed at every opportunity all along the frontier.

In May of 1906 he traveled to Kandahar where he was arrested and subjected to terrible tortures. He would not deny his Christian faith, and he refused to repeat the Muslim word of witness, "There is no God but Allah and Mohammed is the apostle of Allah."

Qazi Abdul Karim's nightmare began when a seventy-pound chain was placed around his neck and a bridle was put in his mouth. Then he was marched the three hundred miles from Kandahar to Kabul, where he was abused all along the way. At Kabul, he again was ordered to repeat the Muslim creed. When he refused, his right arm was cut off with a sword.

Again he was ordered to say it.

But once more he refused to betray his Christian faith.

This time he lost his left arm.

He was ordered to repeat the Muslim word of witness a third time.

When he refused, his captors beheaded him.[4]

Twenty-five years later in 1931, Flora Davidson and Maria Rasmussen were visiting in Mashad, Iran, when an Afghan man came to the home of Dr. and Mrs. Miller for tea, and told of seeing Qazi Abdul Karim's persecution.

"It is many years ago," he said. "I was a boy of ten or twelve at the time, but I have never been able to forget it. I saw a man tortured and hounded to death for his faith in the streets of Kabul.

"He was a Christian," he continued. "The remembrance of the light of the peace on his face remains with me to this day. I can never forget it. Tell me the secret of it."

The man accepted Christ as his Savior and returned to Afghanistan.[5]

There is a little Christian church in Chaman, which today is locked up and unused. Over the fireplace, there is a framed text honoring yet another Afghan martyr, "In memory of Nasrullah Khan who became a Christian on June 11, 1899. He would not deny Christ and was killed by Afghans near Chaman on August 20, 1908. 'He who loses his life for my sake and the gospel's, the same shall find it.' "[6]

Another young Afghan, Mazzaffar, came to the Lord and was adopted by the Patersons, a dedicated missionary couple in Pakistan. Mazzaffar traveled to Kabul and witnessed boldly for Christ. When he was caught, a *mullah* forced acid down his throat saying, "You infidel, we will burn the tongue out of your head and you will speak no more about the Son of God in Afghanistan." He died not long afterwards.[7]

Hosseyn Attish was yet another Afghan native who was murdered for his faith. A native of Herat, he was a student in the University of Kabul during the 1950s. He had been intrigued by Koran passages where he read that Christ even raised the dead, and he longed to find out more about the person who had such power. But at that time it was not possible to buy a Bible in Afghanistan. However, Hosseyn found that one of his Afghan University professors, who was a Communist, had a Persian

New Testament in his library. He asked if he could borrow it, but was refused. The instructor told him it was a very dangerous book. But Hosseyn was bound and determined to get his hands on that book, so he kept on asking the professor over and over again. Finally, he was allowed to take it for one week, on the condition that he would not tell anyone where he got it.

Hosseyn read that Testament every spare moment. He even bought a flashlight, and studied it under the bed covers at night so he would not disturb the others in his dormitory room. When he had to return it at the end of the week, he asked an American Christian professor if he could borrow his Bible. The American was afraid that it might be a trap, and told him he was sorry that he could not let him have the Bible.

But when the professor completed his contract, and was leaving Afghanistan, he told Hosseyn that the Bible was in his desk drawer in the lecture hall if he wanted it. Hosseyn was thrilled to have his own copy of the Scriptures at last!

Hosseyn went on to study for his masters degree at Columbia University in New York, and during one of his vacations he visited a Christian children's camp. There the speaker gave the boys and girls an opportunity to accept Christ as their Savior. Even though he was a graduate student, Hosseyn stood up.

His friends thought that he had misunderstood the speaker, and that he was only standing to be polite. But he insisted that he wanted to show that he was receiving Christ as his Savior, too!

Hosseyn was baptized in New Jersey, and returned to teach at Kabul University. In Afghanistan, he gladly assisted in giving short messages, which were taped and made into gospel recordings (see chapter 7). He also translated a Bible correspondence course from English into Dari. But his desire to promote Christianity eventually got him in trouble with Muslim zealots. Someone poisoned him, and after a three-day fight for life, Hosseyn went to be with his Lord on March 17, 1969.

Afghan converts have not been the only people to die serving the Lord in Afghanistan. Several Christian foreigners have also met violent deaths and have been buried on Afghan soil. During the mid-1950's, a German sports teacher was stabbed and killed by a religious fanatic on a Kabul street. He had only been in the country for six weeks.

More recently, on December 30, 1980, the mutilated bodies

of Erik and Eeva Barendsen were found on their bedroom floor. Their two children, Asko, age five, and Ulla, age three, were found unhurt. But they had been sitting in the blood of their dead parents for almost a day and time will only tell if they will ever be able to recover from the emotional shock.

Erik Barendsen, a native of Holland, and Eeva, a native of Finland, had met during work at the NOOR Eye Hospital in Kabul. Afghanistan had become home, and when the Russians had allowed a handful of foreigners to stay and work in the country, the Barendsens saw no reason to leave. They continued with business as usual.

That, proved to be a mistake. A group of Afghans conducted a rash of murders on December 29 and 30, 1980, to symbolize their distain for the Russians. It was the one year anniversary of the invasion. Mistakenly, the Afghan killers had figured that any foreigners left in the country were somehow tied to the Soviet occupation.

This tragedy stirred the executive committee of the International Assistance Mission (changed from International Afghan Mission) to action. All IAM personnel still in Afghanistan have been temporarily withdrawn until order is restored in the country. God only knows when that will be.

This chapter has only included the story of Afghan Christian martyrs. It is not yet safe to print the exciting story of those believers still living in Afghanistan. Rest assured though, that there are many who are quietly living their Christian testimony in this dangerous land.

It has been said that the blood of martyrs is the seed of God's church. If this is true, a glorious church is going to one day be established in Afghanistan.

Epilogue

"The world lives on hope." [*dunyaw ba omaid khorda shuda.*]
Afghan proverb

One afternoon several years ago, I was driving through the
Afghan countryside with some American friends. We weren't
in any particular hurry, so we stopped the car when we saw an
Afghan farmer plowing his field with a team of oxen. Few
scenes better portray the life of an Afghan peasant, so we each
took several pictures. Little did we realize what was going
through that farmer's mind. He apparently had never seen a
camera before, and for all he knew, the long lenses could have
been gun barrels pointing in his direction. Several times he
glanced over his shoulder at us with a concerned look on his
face.

Then I noticed something else. Before we had arrived on the
scene, all of his plowed furrows were straight. He had set his
sights on a landmark in the distance, and had guided his team in
a direct line to that point. However, when he looked back at us,
the furrow began to weave back and forth. For the first time, I
understood the meaning of Christ's parable about the plow.
Jesus said, "No one, after putting his hand to the plow and
looking back, is fit for the Kingdom of God" (Luke 9:62).

This book has taken a look at the furrows God has been

plowing in Afghanistan—one of the world's most "closed" countries to the gospel. But it was written with Afghanistan's future in mind. Hosea 10:12 says, "Break up your fallow ground for it is time to seek the Lord until He comes to rain righteousness on you." It is my prayer that others will be challenged to pray for the people of Afghanistan and the lost people in the Muslim world. It is my prayer that still others will seek God's will about a possible "tentmaking" ministry in Afghanistan, with the Afghan refugees, or in some other country which is deeply influenced by the pillars of Islam.

Yes, religious liberty is often curtailed in Islamic lands, and if you were to measure missionary success by the number of Christian converts, countries like Afghanistan, Iran, Saudi Arabia, and Libya would sit at the bottom of the list. Some missions experts have gone so far as to label these lands a "green harvest" and raise objections to sending witnesses into resistant Muslim areas. They argue that it is much wiser to expand efforts among receptive peoples where the results in converts are greater.

However, I strongly disagree. Even a green harvest needs care and preparation for the time when it ripens. Outstanding men and women of God have labored in Muslim lands, and others are needed to enter into their labors. Doctor William Miller, who spent forty-three years as a missionary in Iran has said, "The main reason there have been so few Muslims who have come to Christ is not due so much to the peversity of the fish, as it is to the paucity of the fishers." Our Lord has told us to preach the gospel to every creature, and this includes Muslims. In the battle for men's souls, Satan's strongholds need to be attacked. We cannot fail to do so!

The Great Commission is the God-given sequel to Christ's incarnation, crucifixion, and resurrection. It is not a man-made directive, but a divine imperative. Jesus came that we might go, and we can do this in prayer as well as in person.

Dr. Samuel Zwemer spent most of his life as a missionary in Arabia. He was often asked "Why?" His response usually ended with the words of the disciple Peter: "Master, we worked hard all night and caught nothing, but at your bidding I will let down the nets" (Luke 5:5). He believed that if we were obedient to Christ's commission, we too would see a great ingathering from the Muslim world.

The promises in the Word of God were enough for Samuel Zwemer, and they are enough for me. Knowing how God has answered prayer in my own life and the lives of others in Afghanistan, makes me believe that God still has great things in store for the people of this central Asian nation. There is much yet to take place in the story of God's work in this resistant land. The more men and women of dedication who set their sights on God's promises when they plow the ''fields of Afghanistan,'' the faster this stubborn little country will lose its label—''the forbidden harvest.''

Notes

CHAPTER 5
1. 2 Corinthians 5:17

CHAPTER 8
1. Mr. Cleo Shook was the official interpreter for President Eisenhower during his visit to Afghanistan. In a letter to me dated August 17, 1974, Mr. Shook wrote: "Eisenhower did read off the three things we did not get to discuss, and said that Byroade would take up the matter with his (the king's) government. One of the three items listed was the question of the church. The mosque in D.C. was mentioned, as I recall, in the statement. Byroade later on took up the detailed discussion."

CHAPTER 9
1. John Stewart, *The Nestorian Missionary Enterprise* (Trichur, Kerala State, India: Mar Narsai Press, 1961), p. 166.
2. Joseph Wolff, *Researches and Missionary Labours Among Jews, Mohammedans, and Other Sects* (London: 1835), p. 124.
3. Harry Holland, *No Second Spring?* (London: CMS, 1951), p. 15.
4. Fitzroy Maclean, *A Person from England and Other Travellers* (New York: Harper and Brother Pub., 1958), p. 40.
5. Andrew Gordon, *Our India Mission* (Philadelphia: 1886), pp. 102-112.

CHAPTER 10
1. 1 Samuel 22:2
2. Flora M. Davidson, *Missions on the Borders of Afghanistan,* October 1946, p. 7.
3. Ibid., October 1942, p. 1.
4. Ibid.
5. Margaret Ballantyne, *Missions on the Borders of Afghanistan,* January 1954, p. 9.
6. Ibid., p. 6.
7. Flora M. Davidson, *Afghan Prayer Circle,* October 1931, pp. 2, 3.
8. Anna Shipton, *Afghan Prayer Circle,* October 1932, p. 1.

CHAPTER 11

1. Mildred Cable, *Missions on the Borders of Afghanistan,* January 1946, pp. 3, 4.
2. Grubb, "The Need for Nonprofessional Missionaries," p. 11.
3. B. A. Donaldson, *Prairie Girl in Iran and India,* p. 222.
4. Rolla Edwards Hoffman, *Pioneering in Meshed, the Holy City of Iran* (published by himself, 1971), p. 130.
5. Dennis Clark, *Report on Afghanistan,* January 1946, p. 2.
6. Chief secretary to government, NWFP, September 26, 1944.
7. Dennis Clark, *Report on Afghanistan,* January 1946, pp. 9, 13.
8. Ibid., p. 16.
9. Ibid., pp. 16, 17.

CHAPTER 12

1. This was a portion of the University of Wyoming teacher's contract, under its agreement with the U. S. Government.

CHAPTER 15

1. Flora M. Davidson, *Hidden Highway* (Stirling Tract Enterprise, 1944), p. 96.
2. Robert Clark, *Dilawar Khan* (London: Church Missionary Society).
3. Theodore Pennell, *Among the Wild Tribes of the Afghan Frontier* (London: Seeley and Co., Ltd., 1909), pp. 202-210.
4. Ibid., pp. 292, 293.
5. Flora M. Davidson, *Afghan Prayer Circle,* April 1935, pp. 2, 3.
6. Sir Henry Holland, *Frontier Doctor* (London: Hodder and Stoughton, Ltd.), pp. 79-81.
7. A. D. Paterson, *Missions on the Borders of Afghanistan,* October 1946, p. 3.